Horse Sense and Horsemanship

Horse Sense and Horsemanship

Ranking – Partnership – Energy Transfer

Linda Weritz

Copyright of original edition © 2006 by Cadmos Verlag GmbH
Im Dorfe 11, 22956 Brunsbek, Germany
Copyright of this edition © 2008 by Cadmos Books
Translation: Ute Weyer, Anna Schrape
Cover design and layout: Ravenstein + Partner
Typesetting: Nadine Hoenow
Cover photo: Julia Wentscher
Photos: Reto Boltshauser, Michael Maierhofer,
Christiane Slawik, Julia Wetscher

Editorial (English edition): Christopher Long
Printed by: agensketterl Druckerei, Mauerbach

Printed in Austria

ISBN 978-3-86127-928-0
www.cadmos.co.uk

Contents

Contents

Acknowledgements

Many thanks to all my 'instructors', colleagues and students – whether two or four-legged.
A particular thank you to my editor, Anneke Bosse, for her superb help, to Johan Zagers and his team from the dressage stables in Düsseldorf for their excellent support, and to the photographers Christiane Slawik and Julia Wentscher for their wonderful pictures. Another thank you to my translator, Anna Schrape, for her competent work so passionately carried out.
A big thanks also to my family and friends for understanding that I had so little time for them, and for their wonderful support.

For Chiron and Paladin

Linda Weritz

My motivation

In all the years that I have spent with horse people and horses, I have learned one thing above all else: that there are many people all over the world who genuinely love and respect horses.

However, only very few of them may be

considered to be 'true' horse people – proper 'aficionados' – who want to know more about the horse as such and about how it thinks, feels and communicates. These individuals manage to see the world more or less through the eyes of the horse; they become, as it were, a little bit of a horse themselves. Of all the many people involved in all possible aspects of riding and equestrianism, there are so very few who really understand this mysterious animal both intellectually and sensuously and who are able to communicate with it with success.

For over six thousand years humans have dealt with the species 'horse' and it is likely that the problems between human and horse have changed little since horses were first domesticated. It is a shameful thought that in all these 6.000 years of time we have not been able to achieve any significant improvement. It is true that we nowadays have the most modern equipment for horse training at our disposal and that animal rights have been introduced, though at a sad moment in human history. However, most humans and horses still do not enjoy a really happy relationship with one another, and far too many horses are labelled a 'problem'.

If my personal infatuation with horses had not been so strong as a young girl in the 1970s, those years in which I spent so much time in typical German riding schools with their dark iron bar boxes, lack of turn-out, resultant miserable and often disturbed horses, and when I was taught by overly domi-

'Problem horse'? Or rather the result of failed communication between human and animal? (Photo: Slawik)

Harmony between human and horse – that children have, but which is so often lost in adults. (Photo: Wentscher)

nant instructors of dubious competence, I could easily have turned my back on those wonderful creatures. There was, however, all the time the very real idea that it did not have to be that way.

There was another, very different world of horses that intensified my love for them and my desire to spend as much time with them as possible.

I was fortunate enough to spend part of my childhood in the country. Opposite our house was a field with a group of about fifteen ponies, with whom I spent all my spare time. At that time I knew absolutely nothing about horses, but luckily I was not afraid of them either.

It all seemed so full of peace and harmony, which is the most vivid memory I still have of them today. A small stream meandered through the length of the field and at the top end a few trees provided shade. The ponies grazed and drank or brushed the flies out of each other's faces. Sometimes they dozed and at other times the youngsters would romp around. Gradually I summoned up the courage to stroke these small horses and fondle the hair of their necks when they came over to me, and I will never forget how they breathed in the scent of my body and immersed their muzzles in my hair.

Moving to a small town put an abrupt end to those peaceful afternoons. But my love of horses and the wonderful memories of those ponies stayed with me throughout and beyond my riding school years. My desire to train horses with a complete absence of violence and in harmony alone is derived from those experiences of mine as a child. It is my deepest wish to bring that peace and harmony, found on the pony field of my childhood, into today's riding stables in which there are all too many miserable and frustrated people and horses, who have so little of the enjoyment that could be theirs in what they do. You and I have the choice, and it is our decision as people responsible for our own lives whether we want to be unhappy and frustrated with our horses – have fun and enjoy being with them. As a reader, you have already taken an important step by picking up this book and documenting your active interest in developing a fulfilling and harmonious friendship with your horse. By setting a good example in training your horse without violence, using lots of effective praise and possibly in going against accepted practice in your stables, you will be creating a huge difference. You will be showing other people a new method of orientation and will not only be improving the quality of life for your own horse but possibly for those of others, too.

We all want to have sensitive, well-trained horses that are fine in feeling when ridden, that cope well with stress, and that are always willing and happy to work with us. I promise you that this book will show you a straightforward way to get a lot closer to this goal.

'To be able to become a perfect member of a herd of sheep, you must first and foremost be a sheep.'
Albert Einstein

Photo: Wentscher

What turns a love of horses into horsemanship?

And what turns all those women horse lovers into true experts and successful Amazons?

In order to be successful with horses and work with the greatest possible harmony, a trainer requires certain skills. He or she always has to act in such a way that the ranking is clear and needs not be questioned by the horse. Perfect timing when handling and working the horse is just as important as knowledge of the horse's psychology and its way of communicating. I am absolutely convinced that success with horses can be planned. But huge passion and focus are needed, as well as the realisation that we can never know it all. For many years I have been with horses on a daily basis and observed them meticulously, which is what I continue to do today. For me there is no better way to end a day than standing in a field or paddock studying a group of horses. I use the word 'studying' deliberately because I not only observe them, but also at the same time analyse what happens, and why, and what is probably going to happen next. Exactly the same thing, of course, applies to everyday work in riding stables and at competitions. By observing closely on a single evening in any indoor riding school, once you learn to watch critically and train your eye to catch the smallest detail, you can learn so much about horses and their reactions. It is of the utmost importance to find the right trainers, which in itself can be something of a problem …

Watching a herd of horses – informative and just so good. (Photo: Wentscher)

Before such violent reactions occur, horses have usually already signalled their distress – but these signals have not been registered. (Photo: Wentscher)

In almost all cases of real achievement, riders have invested a lot of time and devotion before they take their place on the victory rostrum. Take a wonderful, successful horse expert like Klaus Balkenhol. Neither you nor I will be in any doubt about his success as a rider not being the result of his hacking out twice a week whilst chatting on his mobile.

Developing sensitivity

Horses are emotional animals that communicate mostly on a non-verbal basis and do not plan ahead. Our complex thinking structures make it hard for us to understand the horse's comparatively limited mind (relatively speaking) and to get accustomed to seeing the world through their eyes. From early childhood we have become used to placing our chief emphasis on the spoken word; now suddenly we have to learn to pay attention to the fine or not so fine non-verbal signals given by the horse. Recognising such non-verbal signs and reading them correctly is the essential key to successful communication and understanding.

I am actually quite pleased with all the 'problem horses' that I am able to meet because they show me that there still are horses which are full of life in the way they express themselves and which have not become dulled or given up – unfortunately, there are also plenty of the latter.

The so-called 'problem horses' have usually sent out a number of signals and signs in advance in order to communicate their problems. But the people around them have not recognised these fine warning signs and therefore not reacted. As a result, the horse has been forced to become 'louder' merely in order to be heard – for example, by biting, rearing, bucking, kicking, constantly shying, showing increased nervousness or aggression or resorting to various other 'vices'.

For many people this is good reason to part company with their 'problem horse' and replace it with a new and 'better' one. It is more than likely that after a very short time similar frustrations and misunderstandings will arise…

There is no such thing as a perfect horse, in the same way that there is no such thing as a perfect human being. Each horse presents its own individual challenge due to its own specific character, which the rider must cope with in a skilled and understandable way. For true horse people it is imperative to realise that horses are direct, honest and 'upright' beings which if subjected by us to self-critical examination would always be able to give very good reasons for their behaviour.

Should you now secretly protest, I must assure you quite definitely that the rider is never the victim in his relationship with a horse. Should you think otherwise, you will only be transferring your own potential authority and the responsibility for yourself to your horse. As long as you insist on seeing yourself in the role of 'victim', you will be unable to achieve any significant improvement in your relationship with horses.

Ten guidelines for dealing with the creature 'horse'

1. Every horse ever born is a perfect horse. No horse was ever born with the intention to frustrate, annoy or hurt people.

2. It is solely the influence of people and the reaction of the horse to their treatment by them that compels horses to show resistance, lose their trust or become unfriendly towards people.

3. There are no malicious horses or ones with bad characters. There are many sensitive horses that refuse to be forced to do certain things. There are ill-treated horses that have learnt to avoid people and that are full of fear when in their presence. There are horses that do not trust their owners in situations threatening their survival and that therefore cling to the herd. There are horses that are unable to cope with the tensions their owners have and fight against them. There are horses that have never learnt to trust a human as a friend.

4. All horses are different. There are no two horses with the same mental abilities, the same emotional background or personality. But each and every horse uses almost identical mechanisms in its behaviour with other horses and also with humans for developing relationships of trust that are intimate and harmonious.

5. If you limit your understanding of the social life of horses to behaviour patterns of dominance, hierarchy and submission, you quickly limit the scope of your own personality in your work with horses and in your general handling of them.

6. The keys to a truly successful partnership between human and horse are both respect for the horse and understanding of the emotions and instincts that determine a horse's life.

7. Horses cannot mean everything to us; no matter how strong their love for people is, they remain, just the same, horses with their own very specific needs. They can never truly act as substitute for children or partner – these are expectations they cannot possibly fulfil and which in any case do not do justice to their personality.

8. If we view or treat a horse as a tool for our own vanities and needs, as an object that is to perform according to our demands, we eliminate the original magic and fascination of this noble species and of our bond with it.

9. Should work and contact with a horse lose the joy it once had, it is advisable to evaluate the situation quickly and to consider all those aspects that might help to improve it before serious damage is done to the relationship with the horse or before the frustration becomes permanent.

10. Horses are too precious as comrades in sport and play for the human to descend to using violence, whether in training or in his general handling of them.

Photo: Slawik

A social animal: the horse and its behaviour

Social interaction between horses has become the subject of scientific interest during the last few years – which is lucky for our horses in that they benefit from our newly gained knowledge concerning the social competence and needs of the horse. People learn to understand horses better and how to communicate with them.

Pictures such as this can still be seen, but fortunately they are becoming less frequent. (Photo: Wentscher)

Our knowledge of the social hierarchy existing in free herds, the effects of domestication, and our research into horses' specific social needs has been deepened, and this has led to constant improvements in the conditions in which horses are kept when in human care.

Life in the herd

There are at least two different forms of possible constellations within free-living herds. The one most familiar to us is the family group. This consists of a leading stallion and usually not more than two or three brood mares with their offspring of the last few years. One of the older mares, the alpha-mare with the greatest experience, generally knows the best feeding grounds, watering places, where to find valuable minerals and where best to roll, and it is she who decides when, where and for how long the herd grazes and drinks. Due to her high rank, she can isolate the stallion from the lower-ranked mares that are also in season and ensure that she is the first to become pregnant again. By being the first to mate with the stallion, she secures the advantage that her foal will be the first to be born the following spring and thus will have an advantage over the other foals born later.

In larger herds, instead of a rigid hierarchy among the individual members, smaller groups tend to form with either a higher or lower status within the group as a whole and among whose members the differences in rankings are minimal or even non-existent.

Should a herd be threatened by predators or by other stallions, the leading stallion will take it upon himself to protect the herd by driving it away from the danger. I use the term 'leading stallion' deliberately, because it is not uncommon in larger herds to find two stallions which, however, have their own very clear ranking established between them. The leading stallion of the herd will cover most mares and predominantly provide for their safety, while the lower-ranked stallion will cover the remaining lower-ranked mares and be more involved than the leading stallion in raising the offspring. There are studies showing that mares will be more likely to leave a herd if it only has one stallion, and that the most stable form of herd is one with several stallions.

The second type of herd, the so-called youngster or bachelor herd, is made up of young stallions together with other stallions that as yet have no herd of their own. In their original family herd, the leading stallion either no longer tolerated them or they simply left because in the bachelor herd they can find many more potential companions to play and tussle with. The bachelor group also offers protection and social interaction to former leading stallions that have lost their mares to another stallion.

These bachelor groups usually live in close proximity to herds with mares, constantly awaiting the opportunity to find straying mares to mate with, or to cover them secretly while the leading stallion's attention is distracted, or even steal them from the group. Therefore, these groups fluctuate considerably, especially during mating seasons.

In wild herds, the leading mare determines the course of everyday life, while the job of the stallion is to protect the group. (Photo: Slawik)

The so-called bachelor herd offers young stallions protection and gives them the opportunity to develop their skills. (Photo: Slawik)

The role of the stallion

The main task of a stallion in the family group is to keep the group together by permanently watching over the mares and their foals. On the one hand, he has to see to it that he does not lose any mares who might simply wander off; on the other, he has to protect the herd from predators or from other stallions intending to steal mares or secretly cover them while he is distracted. His success as leading stallion is defined by how well he is able to prevent such surreptitious copulation. To do this, he circles his herd at a distance of about ten to fifteen metres, and during periods of rest he rarely sleeps, just dozes. For this reason, the size of a herd is limited because the larger the herd, the less he will be able to protect his group against other stallions trying to penetrate it. Especially when the mares come into season for the first time after foaling, about six to twelve days later, a time when they are particularly fertile, he must be vigilant in fending off other stallions.

The stallion generally drives his mares directly or at an angle from behind, while the alpha-mare leads the group from the front. While driving them forwards, he holds his head and neck low, raising his nose so that neck and head almost form a straight line. With a movement coming from the neck, he now weaves his head snakelike from side to side or up and down. His pulled-back ears give him a mildly to severely aggressive expression. The high knee action characteristic of stallions is maintained, despite the lowered head. This is the so-called driving position that the stallion uses to drive his mares forward when danger threatens. He also uses this position when making the herd change direction or to drive his own youngsters or undesired rival stallions away from the herd. If one or even several new mares are to be integrated into the herd, he will drive them forward in this way for up to three days in order to make his claim to 'ownership' undisputed and also to establish the ranking, whilst the other mares in his herd carry on grazing undisturbed. Foals as well that have got lost or have escaped from the herd are brought back by the leading stallion in the same manner.

While several studies claim that the most stable form of herd constellation is one with a second, lower-ranked stallion that is only allowed to cover about one-quarter of the mares but must also help to establish the inner security and stability of the herd, oth-

Typical driving posture of a stallion: neck and head are extended forwards and form one line, the ears are drawn back. (Photo: Slawik)

er authors state that in a herd with two stallions there are frequent aggressive confrontations between them and therefore a lower number of births. Surveys carried out amongst wild horses in the Camargue have shown that foal mortality as a result of predators is reduced by up to 20% when a second stallion is present.

Generally, the leading stallion has a very close relationship with his higher-ranked mares and interacts in a playful and friendly way with his offspring, both male and female, until they reach maturity. Some authors suggest that the sporting or even aggressive ranking manifestations of a stallion within his herd are intended as interval training for his offspring and as a way of keeping them fit. The physically weaker youngsters in particular are exercised individually in order to help them to become more supple, develop stronger hindquarters and learn how to take the offensive.

Due to the male sex hormone testosterone, stallions are less timid than mares or youngsters. (Photo: Slawik)

In the event of sudden danger, the stallion positions himself between the cause of the threat and his herd in order to shield them. His greatly increased readiness to display aggression, triggered by the male sex hormone testosterone, makes him less timid and less fearful than the mares and the youngsters. At the same time, with his head well lowered and with the oscillating movements proceeding from the base of the neck, he drives the herd away from the focus of danger.

This behaviour can also be seen when a foal is newly born into the herd. By driving the other curious herd members away from the mare and her foal, the stallion gives both of them the time and peace they need to bond. Should a stallion want to cover one of his mares that he has identified as prepared to mate, he will also sometimes drive her a bit away from the herd using the same gestures. As soon as a rival stallion approaches the herd too closely, looking for mares of his own, the leading stallion will try to drive him off and frighten him with an aggressive charge.

An exchange will follow in the form of a ritualised posturing, an attempt to impress which often develops no further, for a serious fight involves a tough 'cost versus benefit calculation' for both sides. On the one hand, the determining factor in the fight for important resources – whether a mare, some lush grazing ground or any other object of interest to horses – is the value or importance of the resources in question to the individual stallion, combined with the open question as to his ability to defend them in future. But possible injuries and subsequent wound infections are the other side of the equation. The 'cost versus benefit calculation' can be vividly illustrated by two possible scenarios: a confrontation between two leading stallions, each with his own herd, and in contrast, the confrontation between a leading stallion and a single bachelor stallion. In the first case, a true fight with serious injuries, possibly leaving the wounded stallion exposed to death through predators, would be a pure waste of energy. Instead, impressive posturing and eventually ritualised fights that are not aimed at inflicting injury determine the ranking between the two herds.

One of the two stallions will finally move his herd away or, for example, at a watering place let the other horses drink first, without any serious injury inflicted on either side.

In the second scenario of a leading stallion meeting a young bachelor stallion, there is more probability of a serious fight: on the one hand because the lone intruder has little to lose and a lot to gain, namely, the entire herd for himself; on the other hand, for the simple reason that the leading stallion has so much to lose, namely, all his mares and foals. Since the leading stallion will defend his herd with all the aggression he can possibly muster, these fights are rarely successful for the intruder – except in those cases when the leading stallion is ill or too old to fight.

Stallion meets stallion – more ritual than fight

The interactions between stallions usually consist of ritualised displays combining threatening and imposing postures.

Thus actual fights and the risk of subsequent injuries can be avoided or at least minimised.

In many cases, stallions display ritualised posturing – serious fights between two stallions are the exception. (Photo: Slawik)

Power macho: often the appearance of the stallion alone is enough to scare off intruders. (Photo: Slawik)

These rituals are made up of repeated sequences of posturing intended to impress:

1. Each rival standing and staring at the other, accompanied sometimes by neighing, tail switching and the stomping of hooves.

2. High body tension, with the neck well arched and the tail raised, the powerful and forcible placing of the hooves in collected walk, piaffe and passage, erection or even masturbation, and the passing of urine and faeces on top of other droppings in order to demonstrate ownership.

The high body tension of the stallion serves importantly to impress the rival. (Photo: Wentscher)

If neither yields, the aggression between two stallions will intensify during the course of their confrontation – with sudden well-aimed kicks included. (Photo: Slawik)

3. On approaching each other, an intensive inhaling of the rival's smell at his nostrils, neck, flanks, penis and anal region.

4. Grunting and squealing as acoustic threats, 'body checks' and kicks with the forelegs.

About half the encounters between wild stallions end after the first ritual of staring, when each party returns to its own herd and emphatically drives it together to demonstrate its claim to leadership over its harem. Many encounters last only a few minutes, but dramatic confrontations can continue for up to 90 minutes, during which single sequences of the rituals described above are repeatedly performed.

Should the opponents fail to separate, the intensity of the aggression will increase and become more physical. Without warning, one of the rivals can suddenly kick out with well-aimed attacks of either fore- or hindlegs, or he may bite.

Thereupon, one of them might flee or, failing that, fight back, and subsequently serious fighting with rearing, biting, kicking, mounting, 'body checks' and wrestling is possible, which is interrupted by fighting rituals until a clear winner is established.

Most confrontations occur because of too great a proximity between two different herds or because of challenging attacks on the part of bachelor stallions that want to test the leading stallion's ability to defend.

Hormone influences and sexual maturity of stallions

Before the first weeks of their lives have passed, young colts will be trying to mount their mothers or attempt something similar, but not until he is about 28 months of age is a stallion considered to be sexually mature.

Studies of wild horses have shown that 17 in 22 males leave the herd after the birth of the next sibling. This may be due to a shortage of resources triggering an increase in aggressively motivated behaviour (agonistic) within the group, so that individuals or several herd members leave together in order to find other grazing areas. The behaviour of young stallions after leaving the original herd undergoes two phases. During the first one they engage mainly in social play and friendly actions which stabilise the bonding within the group of stallions. In the second phase they attempt to establish a hierarchy amongst themselves, and the highest-ranking stallion will attempt to take over a herd of mares for himself. Very often, however, a clear ranking does not fully develop in bachelor herds.

Flight, too, has to be learned – here these colts at play are training for it. (Photo: Wentscher)

Usually, no clear hierarchy can be detected in the playful interactions of young stallions. (Photo: Slawik)

petition, the higher the stallion's testosterone and adrenaline levels within the family or bachelor group, and with them his aggression and fertility. This also works in the reverse situation when a former leading stallion joins a bachelor group because he has lost his herd to a rival. His testosterone and adrenaline levels sink and there is usually a temporary phase of depression due to the hormonal and social changes.

These facts contradict the common belief that stallions always have to be kept isolated because they are 'by nature' aggressive. Aggression and fertility in stallions are influenced by testosterone and adrenaline levels and fluctuate with changes in external stimuli.

Stallions do not necessarily have to be kept in solitary confinement. (Photo: Slawik)

The status of a stallion is closely connected to its hormone levels, especially testosterone. Testosterone levels increase gradually with age up to the point when a stallion takes over his own herd. With some stallions, the levels are linked to the size of the herd. The production of the hormones testosterone and adrenaline are influenced positively by the presence of rival stallions: that is, the greater the com-

The role of the mare

The leading mare in the herd is one of the older mares, she who has the most experience. She leads the group and determines its daily schedule. Should the herd be attacked and flight is not possible, she and the other highly ranked mares will help the stallion to defend the group, which in turn forms a circle, protecting the foals and yearlings in the middle.

The mares often have a close social relationship with each other and also form a tight and long-standing bond with their daughters; such close contact is not possible with their male offspring, who often leave the group on reaching sexual maturity. Only when food resources become scarce does it happen that up to 30% of the mares might leave the group. In such cases small groups of mares, related to each other or bound together by friendship, will leave the original herd and are usually quickly 'adopted' by a new stallion.

Wild mares have very highly developed maternal instincts. Orphan foals are adopted and raised as their own. Young mares that as yet do not have foals of their own help to raise the offspring (altruistic behaviour) and in this way learn to become good mothers themselves. Mares protect one another, keep heavily pregnant mares in the middle of their group and are protected in return when the birth of their own foals is imminent.

The close social bond between the mares in a herd also serves to protect heavily pregnant mares from the attacks of predators. (Photo: Wentscher)

This stallion knows his daughter and is unlikely to become sexually aroused by her when she reaches sexual maturity.
(Photo: Slawik)

Mothers develop an unerring instinct as to whether foals and youngsters are just rollicking around or, instead, are going too far and violating the established rules of hierarchy. Play is lovingly tolerated, whereas any infringement of rankings will be punished firmly and uncompromisingly. As a rule, grazing mares walk ahead of their foals, but when the herd moves on or is faced with a dangerous situation, the mares protectively surround the foals.

Due to the presence of close bonding within a herd, the risk of inbreeding between a stallion and his daughters is slim. Although incest will certainly occur sometimes, most stallions know their daughters and will not be sexually aroused by them.

In wild herds. the daughters usually leave the group either when they reach sexual maturity or when another stallion steals them. In this latter special case, the leading stallion will not try all too hard to prevent it. Even a take-over of the entire herd by another stallion is possible. This is the reason why herd constellations with two stallions do exist and why this gives the herd a certain stability: the double gene pools will prevent inbreeding.

The role of foals and yearlings

In natural herds youngsters are the least aggressive and through submissive behaviour mostly give the older horses to understand that they are not interested in conflict or competitive confrontations.

Foals play a lot and explore their surroundings with curiosity whenever the herd grazes or rests on grassland with wide, open vistas. But when danger threatens, the foals and youngsters will immediately rush to their mothers for protection.

When at play, a hierarchy is not initially important. Only later, when the youngsters are one or two years old and their games have become rougher, will they develop a hierarchy, which is not static, however.

Fillies do not take part in ranking confrontations because they inherit their status in the herd from their mothers. As long as the filly runs with her mother she has her mother's rank, and when she is older she will be placed immediately behind her mother. If a mare has several daughters from previous years they often maintain a close bond, with the oldest and most experienced usually ranked highest. Thus, not just inherited rank but also age, experience and physical fitness are important factors in determining a foal's place in the herd. However, nature does not work as simply as to have merely these factors alone responsible for the ranking within the herd. There are always individuals that will show special leadership qualities, and others who fall below their inherited rank.

No matter how curious foals may be, as soon as there is any sign of danger they will cling to their mother's side. (Photo: Wentscher)

Photo: Slawik

Why ranking is important

In order to be able to understand inferiority and submission as essential elements of a successful ranking system, we need first to take a good look at the reasons why they exist.

The structuring of life in a group has proved beneficial for many mammals (human beings included). This is mainly because protection from predators and other threatening elements functions better and more efficiently in a well-organised group. Horses can graze relatively peacefully within a herd because individual guards keep watch and will alarm the rest of the herd immediately as soon as any possible danger threatens.

The organisation of life in a group, however, also presents a range of challenges to the individual members. It is not possible, for example, for everyone, democratically, to have the same access to limited resources, such as the best feeding places or a favourite sexual partner. Not every thirsty horse, for instance, can be the first to drink at a spring or watering place. In order to prevent banal situations like these from turning into chaos, the herd establishes a ranking order to regulate its inner structure. It would be exceedingly counterproductive for a herd if, in similar everyday situations, ferocious fights broke out each time; firstly, this would attract predators that would try to take advantage of the chaos and attack, with good prospects of success, or, secondly, it would expose the horses to a high risk of injury. Both scenarios would result in a weakening of the whole group and, subsequently, of the entire species.

Therefore, throughout evolution, as the driving force in the survival of the species, mammals living in social groups have developed signs and gestures of aggression, submission and sympathy that allow a clear understanding between the individual group members.

These signs enable not only the establishment of a clearly defined hierarchy, but also the development of friendships and partnerships. For our horses as well, this ranking

This foal indicates its submission to the stallion by 'snapping'. (Photo: Wentscher)

guarantees an orderly everyday routine that is as peaceful as possible. Horses are generally content with their status within a group, as long as it is clearly defined.

In the past, it was assumed that just one dominant horse controlled the whole herd

One stands guard and the others can devote themselves to grazing or resting – for potential prey like horses permanently exposed to the danger of predators, an important factor for survival is living in a group. (Photo: Slawik)

Living in a herd – for good reason!

The most important aim of all animals and thus of our horses as well is to ensure the survival and reproduction both of the individual and of the species.

Horses form well-established, stable groups with clearly defined roles and responsibilities in order to optimise the safety of each member and his chances of survival. Furthermore, the precise social organisation seems above all to depend on the type and nature of the environment. To illustrate this, we will now look more closely at the social structures of two other equidae, both close relatives of the horse.

The Grevy's zebra (*equus grevy*) and the African wild donkey (*equus asinus*) are particularly territorial animals. One stallion will perhaps occupy the same territory for many years and defend it with the utmost aggression against intruding rivals. Should a mare enter a stallion's territory, there is no reason at all to fight. The mare and the stallion can mate without any interference from other stallions because it is exclusively the home territory of the male that determines 'ownership' of the mares. This type of social organisation, territorially structured reproduction, probably derives from early primitive equidae still living in woodlands.

Moreover, it is of interest to note that neither Grevy's zebras nor the African wild donkey possesses the social instinct of form-

and its organisation. This role was accorded to the leading stallion as the chauvinist patriarchal leader of the group. More intensive research, however, came to the conclusion that it was the alpha-mare that tended to have the dominant position within the herd and that it was she who decided when and where the herd eats and drinks. Today, however, the picture is even more complex; the idea of one dominant leader of the herd has been replaced by that of a far more differentiated herd structure involving differing social responsibilities and changing hierarchies in changing contexts.

Amongst various zebra breeds the type and nature of the environment determines the varying organisation of herd behaviour. (Photo: Boltshauser)

ing long-lasting relationships. Adult individuals either live alone or join together in loose groupings that can change from one hour to the next. The only more lasting bond is between a mother and her foal.

The horse, the Plains zebra and Mountain zebra, however, form herds of several mares with their offspring and usually one stallion, and these herds remain unchanged over many years.

The difference in social structure amongst the various species is founded in their different mating habits. Mating habits, in turn, depend on the availability of resources like water and food. Grevy's zebras and African wild donkeys defend their territories where-

as none of the other zebra subspecies or, indeed, horses has any fixed territories but is constantly on the move, looking for adequate water and food.

Hence, the formation of family groups offers on the one hand a possible social structure, when there is no reference to any defined territory, but they are also a necessity since males then cannot 'own' potential sexual partners merely because they enter their home territory. Seen the other way round, the arrangement of social structures within the group is the basis for the group being able to move freely in order to find new grazing grounds and adequate sources of water.

Forming friendships and social bonds is rooted in a horse's instinct. (Photo: Wentscher)

Living in an organised herd enables horses to build social relationships and successfully reproduce, despite the need to be constantly on the move in search of food. Breeding behaviour is thus independent of territory.

It is therefore not surprising that horses instinctively form lifelong relationships with other members of their species. This instinct is developed so strongly that it is also present in domesticated horses. Under our modern conditions horses will develop very close friendships, for the most part completely independently of sexual behaviour, for example, between same-sex companions and even between horse and goat, goose, dog or members of other species.

In conclusion, we can say that horses have developed a social structure within a herd in order firstly to assure reproduction in non-territorial groups, and secondly to develop and preserve the gene pool of the herd as best as possible. In the long term, the advantages of this socially organised lifestyle are greater than the disadvantages.

Advantages of life in a herd

• In a group there is a higher number of potential recipients wary of danger and, therefore, the approach of predators is registered earlier, which helps to protect all individual herd members.

In addition, the risk of danger is distributed over a larger number of animals so that the chances of survival are greater for each individual. At the same time, lush grazing areas can be more easily detected

or even rediscovered and this improves the survival prospects for all.
• If a predator focuses on a single animal within the herd, the others can attack and drive it off. Should the herd flee, the predator will lose track of the chosen victim more quickly in the tumult.
• Under certain circumstances, the leading stallion will tolerate the presence of another stallion. Co-operation between two stallions offers better protection of the herd from other rival stallions or predators.
• The gene pool of the herd is better protected because other mothers can adopt orphaned foals, and the mares support each other while raising foals and youngsters. Young mares also help to watch over and educate the foals, thus gaining valuable experience in learning to be 'good' mothers themselves.

Disadvantages of life in a herd
• Foals can be injured or even killed by other herd members if, for example, panic breaks out or there is fighting for resources.
• Aggressive competition for available resources becomes more intense and can only be successfully compensated for by a defined social structure within the herd.
• Contagious disease can spread throughout the herd more easily due to the close contact.

Safety in numbers: in the tumult of flight a predator will soon lose track of a chosen victim. (Photo: Slawik)

Social organisation of the herd

To enable the social organisation of a herd to function, certain mechanisms have to obtain which guarantee the strong hold that the group exerts on its members – mechanisms that preserve and stabilise the individual relationships within the group.

It is of the utmost importance to the stability of the group that each herd member has a clearly defined status. The risk of injury

The ranking of each member of the herd is determined by his social competence. (Photo: Slawik)

for each individual is drastically reduced when actual physical fighting is replaced by mere gestures or threats of such, like biting, kicking or pushing aside.

The position of each herd member is determined by at least two factors: on the one hand by social competence, that is, the ability to form friendships – for example, through taking the initiative with mutual grooming (allogrooming) and protecting a partner from other herd members or invaders (altruistic behaviour). On the other hand, it is also behaviour motivated by aggression (agonistic) that likewise plays an important role in establishing a hierarchy.

Aggression is only effective when it is acknowledged by the receiving party – not every horse sending aggressive signals has a high rank. (Photo: Slawik)

In this context it is important to realise that not every horse that 'claims' to be the boss is, in fact, the boss. The horse at whom aggressive behaviour is aimed must confirm that the message has been understood.

Much research of the past concentrates mainly on the expression of aggressive behaviour to explain the theory of herd rankings being the basis of herd organisation. Many authors, indeed, consider not only the frequency of aggressive signals, but also take exact count of which horse is the target of aggressive acts from other members, in what situation and how often. This explains why so much thought concerning horse herds and groups is focused on rankings, seen as a pecking order or as hierarchy through domination. This concept is most likely based on a German study carried out in 1913 investigating the pecking order of chickens – a theory that for decades was applied to all possible other animal species because it seemed to explain social organisations in a simple, neat and concise manner.

However, if we take a closer look at the social life of horses, we cannot accept such a purely dominance-orientated approach, because this would mean that horses have to compete with each other continuously, and this, in such a form, is clearly not the case. There is certainly competition for food resources within a herd and amongst different groups, especially under unfavourable climatic conditions. But, generally, horses do not have to fight over a few blades of

Pictures like this show that the organisation of life in a herd is a lot more complex than that of a simple 'pecking order'. (Photo: Slawik)

grass or over dwindling water resources, and in the wild there are not many tracks so narrow as to necessitate a confrontation as to who should pass along it first. Therefore, the view of a herd structure orientated purely around aggression and hierarchy is simplistic and, because of this lack of precision, scientifically incorrect. Furthermore, it has not been confirmed that only the biggest or

Social bonds are essential factors for the successful functioning of a herd structure. (Photo: Slawik)

Social organisation of horses under human care

Domesticated horses kept in stables, fields and paddocks can rarely be observed in a family group. They are usually individuals from totally different backgrounds and of varied age, size and weight. It is therefore all the more surprising that these horses, if conditions make it possible, often form close, lifelong bonds with other companions. Their need for social interaction is plain to see. On the other hand, the likelihood of aggressive confrontation within the group is higher, because in fields or paddocks the possibility of fleeing or of joining other groups is very limited or completely impossible. Due to the reduced living space available which the horses have to share with each other, a space far too confined from their point of view, aggressive conflicts are much more common.

Likewise, conditions of temporary or constant isolation from other horses lead to a greater tendency towards aggression, because isolated horses cannot learn or practise social interaction sufficiently. The aggression in these cases stems almost exclusively from social insecurity (deprivation).

If on top of that a person then introduces artificial competition, for example, by walking into a field with treats or a bucket of food, or when several horses have to walk past each other through the narrow stable

heaviest horses or those who often attack others are necessarily the leading horses of the herd. Several studies have shown that animals with aggressive tendencies are no more intelligent or talented than other more peaceful individuals.

We can therefore state that aggressive behaviour is not the main factor for the successful organisation of a herd structure that does not naturally have many daily conflicts in need of solving. Thus, we can assume that it is far more likely that the behavioural patterns, which minimise aggression (submission) and enhance social competence in terms of friendships and family bonds, are the determining factors that keep a herd together.

passageway, aggressive behaviour will be triggered more often. Hierarchies based on dominance are therefore more a product of our modern stable management or of the approach taken by so many people of seeing the social structure amongst horses exclusively in terms of a 'pecking order'.

It is rooted in their very nature that horses want to develop friendly relationships and have a readiness to follow others. As a rule, they have a strong feeling and natural gift for establishing and maintaining close, long-lasting bonds. It is this characteristic that has made some researchers suggest we should turn from focusing on the aggressive and submissive actions within a herd and concentrate more on all actions directed at establishing peaceful contacts and social bonding.

When observing several horses kept in a group on a field or paddock under three specific aspects, it soon becomes clear that the hierarchy is not linear from top to bottom. Horse 1 may dominate horse 2, but not horse 3. This leads to a fairly complex herd structure, especially when we look at the hierarchy in specific situations: who is the first to drink? Who walks into the shelter first? Who protects the herd from invaders, for example, from dogs?

It is extremely interesting to study a herd or small group of horses using these criteria. Some scientists have also found out that among horses there are those who send emotional signals more often, whereas others send fewer but are all the more often at the

This expression of insecurity can be caused by socially determined problems. (Photo: Slawik)

Lack of space increases aggressive behaviour. (Photo: Wentscher)

receiving end. This is yet another important consideration to be taken into account when studying horses and evaluating their social competence.

The stallion under human care

We have already described the 'normal' or ideal life of a stallion (see as from page 20) – and in the light of that knowledge it will become immediately obvious to us that life for a stallion in the solitary confinement of a stable is utterly different in almost every way. Wherever stallions are kept, the conditions of their surroundings should deviate from those specific needs already described as little as possible, though we have to remember that not every wild stallion will manage to lead a herd of his own. Evolution selects the most intelligent and strongest (in character as in body) for this task in order to allow the best genes of a species to be reproduced as often as possible.

Stallions that have no contact with mares apart from specific breeding procedures very often develop difficult behaviour patterns, because they are able neither to learn nor practise social skills. As highly social animals, whose gentle tenderness can take on very touching forms, they are not made for life in isolation. Therefore, many stallions kept without a herd or even without any intensive contact with other horses, develop a high level of frustration that finds expression in an often considerably increased aggression.

For reasons of convenience or even vanity, people subject stallions (and other horses, too, of course) to a life of social deprivation without allowing them any possibility of interacting with companions or living in tune with their natural purpose, so they soon become 'anti-social' individuals.

Yet, living within the context of a hierarchy is a genetic instinct rooted in a stallion's brain, and only in extreme situations would he go against the decision of a skilled and experienced leading mare, or challenge an aggressive, strong and brave young stallion whose time has come to take over the herd, especially if his own strength is fading. It is possible, though not always easy, to allow domesticated stallions to lead a natural life, as long as in the past, as foals and youngsters within a herd, they had the opportunity to experience and learn social skills. For the domesticated stallion such a herd can consist of a few mares when these are to be mated, or of other stallions and geldings. The previous experiences of the stallion are the key to success. If he was given the opportunity to learn herd behaviour and social skills, he should be able to live within a group without presenting a risk of injury to the other horses.

If that is not the case, patient, sensitive and competent training can enable the stallion to learn or relearn these skills, especially when he can be together with other experienced and dominant horses that help him to practise learning the rules of living within a group.

Many stallions are fed a protein and energy-rich diet in order to make them look good and mate successfully. This diet makes them hugely fit and strong. But they seldom have the chance to work off their energy in a positive way, and that again can lead to a build-up of unreleased power and thus to frustrations which in turn result in a higher risk of injury for other horses and people. Stallions that are not registered for breeding should not be used for this purpose, for there are already enough horses living under impossibly difficult conditions whose physical and psychological defects greatly reduce their value to people. Charismatic, 'beautiful' and healthy horses with a pleasant character can usually expect to lead a better life than 'screwed-up' animals of doubtful origins.

Keeping stallions and geldings together can work well but can also be problematic. A gelding is an 'artificial' animal, created by man, that does not exist in the wild – thus a stallion is not genetically prepared to deal with the social behaviour of this sexless horse. If a stallion is familiar with geldings and their specific behavioural characteristics, the chances of successful and peaceful co-existence in the long run are much greater.

Stallions are highly social animals – but when not kept under reasonably natural conditions they can become very aggressive. (Photo: Slawik)

Horses and humans in social interaction

> '*Problems can never be solved by the same way of thinking that created them.*'
>
> *Albert Einstein*

Most horses, according to my observation, never have a clearly established ranking order in their relationships with 'their' humans. This is unsatisfactory for both sides and tends to promote the development of serious problems.

The fact that so often everything appears to be going well is, on the one hand, due to the noble character of horses (they can be very 'forgiving', although they never forget) and, on the other, because many people simply do not realise how undefined their ranking relationship with their horse is. Often not until extreme situations crop up – for example, when loading – are problems revealed that disclose an undetermined hierarchy. In such cases the erratic behaviour of the horse will be assigned to his specific character or to previous experiences and, with that, the connection to the present interaction between human and horse is overlooked.

This is certainly not intentional! It is perfectly understandable when we consider how little we are taught about the communication and behaviour of the equine species. It is not a coincidence that many horse lovers nowadays turn to alternative riding and training methods because the average (German) riding school, unfortunately, almost exclusively teaches and promotes only the more technical aspects of riding.

Many riders and horse owners consciously or unconsciously humanise their horses, and each applies his own acquired behavioural patterns to his horse and lives them out accordingly. I have the impression that in the case of many women in particular, it almost suits them to have to argue constantly with their horse (in a more or less friend-

In extreme situations like loading, an undetermined ranking between human and horse becomes very obvious. (Photo: Slawik)

ly fashion) and 'call it to order'. It is also very convenient for us to be able to live out our mothering instincts to the full when caring for our horses which, indeed, have been torn from their natural environment, tamed and then kept in functional stables for us. These horses, made as good as completely helpless in this way, now depend entirely on our care, which as such is not a big problem as long as in the end a horse is able to remain a horse. If you have been able to observe horses in the wild, it becomes very clear to you that they have no need of us for their psyche or their survival – but we certainly need them.

And that's a good thing. If we did not value horses so much, only a very few of them would have survived the age of industrialisation to be admired nowadays in zoos. Today there are so many horses and different breeds in the world, more so probably than ever before in the almost 60 million years of evolutionary development of *equus caballus*, our domesticated horse.

It is always the greatest pleasure for me to discover that there are horses in all the most remote corners of this planet. But it is disheartening to have to see that all too often people and horses are not happy together because they do not understand each other enough in order to develop a harmonious and successful relationship that will give both parties enjoyment and satisfaction.

Your horse does not know how expensive the travelling boots were and, accordingly, it will not be 'grateful' for them. (Photo: Wentscher)

All of us want to try to have a harmonious and close relationship with our horses – with the possible exception of the rare type of person, hopefully soon extinct, who gets his dubious satisfaction from sitting on a creature that is tense, trembling with fear and degraded to the status of a slave. Most men and women involved with horses, however, do not have the urge to dominate and, instead, apply the principle of 'Be nice to me and I'll be nice to you'.

This principle is certainly good and laudable, but a very important aspect of horse psychology is thereby omitted: it is essential for the survival of a horse to know who is responsible for the survival of its mini-herd consisting of human and horse. Although horses are now kept in a safe stable-management environment and the sabre-toothed tiger has long since become extinct, and although all other potential predators, with the exception of the human, have disappeared from the scene, horses remain what they have always been, namely, flight animals, with all their original instincts still absolutely intact.

Life-threatening predators have now been replaced by tractors, bins, sheets of plastic, flowerpots, birds suddenly flying up, and any other potentially 'dangerous' object or noise. The horse uses them, so to speak, to train its instincts and keep them intact.

It is useful to recall that horses have only been domesticated for around 6.000 years, and in spite of their enormous ability to adapt they could easily go back to their wild roots at any time. Thanks to their highly developed senses and their undamaged instincts, they would still have a very real chance of surviving.

I wish to advocate the position that the importance of these undamaged instincts be fully acknowledged and allowed, instead of the usual reaction of annoyance shown by so many people whenever a horse starts or shies. When you think of how many horses there are that know nothing in the world other than their stable, the stable passageway and indoor riding school, but that if these very horses were set free they could find their way back to their original life out in the wild and revert to their basic way of living with full success, you have to admit that it is a fantastic achievement!

A horse is actively preoccupied with its own survival, and its well-developed senses help him with this. It does not know that its natural predators no longer exist. We as people don't have the means to convey intellectually to the horse that its life is not in danger. But we have other ways with which to turn a scared and jumpy horse into a 'bombproof' companion.

Firstly, we have to understand that a horse in a naturally formed herd or in any other form of group does not live in a democracy ('Now let's have a vote on whether we want to flee or not'). The decisions concerning the behaviour of the entire herd are left to one or at most to a very few individuals that have

The horse has always been and still is a flight animal, and in any and every situation it needs to know who is responsible for its survival. (Photo: Wentscher)

the required experience and routine and that are the most capable, predominantly due to their age, of conveying this self-assurance and self-confidence to the others.

In addition, horses in a herd are not persuaded, appeased or admonished to 'please stay calm and sensible'. A sense of safety is perceived by the herd through their awareness of the controlled confidence and active competence of the high-ranking members who pass this on via emotional transmission.

ioural pattern, for the horse will be confirmed in its fear of pain and subsequently become even more tense. Furthermore, it creates an utterly confusing situation for the horse: after attempting to assume responsibility for 'its' own mini-herd, it is punished for doing just exactly that. It is obvious that such actions will hardly improve the level of friendship and trust between human and horse. The horse may be intimidated by the violent action, but physical punishment will not make it recognise us as a wise, higher-ranked leader and friend.

Praising and petting a nervous, jumpy horse will only reinforce this behaviour unnecessarily. (Photo: Wentscher)

Perfect manners from the very beginning

However, if you should visit any ordinary riding school on any ordinary evening, you will be presented with a very different picture. Experienced horse owners who have been riding since their youth try to tell their horses in an 'intellectual' manner that they do not need to feel fear. Through their well-meant actions, however, they only reinforce the horse's frightened behaviour.

The second frequently seen variation on the theme is a horse being physically punished for shying or showing fear. This will only serve to intensify the undesired behav-

Many people try to make friends with horses or to preserve a friendship by feeding them with treats. Often the following situation occurs: a horse stands in its stable or paddock; as soon as a person approaches, the horse walks towards him, expecting a lovely treat; the person is pleased that the horse appears to be so trusting and friendly and empties the contents of his pocket, feeding the horse from the hand.

For the horse, not only receiving the treat is important. It also learns in most cases that it can enter someone's personal space without asking and will even be rewarded for it. This kind of situation just does not exist among horses.

Feeding from the hand is a problem: the horse enters someone's personal space without asking and thus proves itself to be of higher rank. (Photo: Slawik)

People, as well, do not like it when a person they do not know stands too close (for example, at a supermarket check-out). Infringement of our protective or personal space by strangers usually creates fear and aggression, although often unconsciously so. When we meet someone for the first time, it is important to keep a certain physical distance while establishing contact, because otherwise we quickly develop a negative attitude. This is very plain to see when we imagine the discomfort of being in a crowded lift or train. The enforced physical proximity is disturbing and oppressive. Eye contact can be seen as aggression, so most people stare at the floor or walls. Our pulse rises when the physical distance to strangers is too short, skin conductance is reduced and the body sends out stress signals.

Only family members and friends or people with our express permission – for example, doctors, carers or hairdressers – are allowed to move in close proximity to our bodies and to touch us without it being perceived as threatening or unpleasant. Interestingly, these rules of preserving our individual distance break down when we meet dogs, cats or horses. Little girls intrepidly ask if they can 'stroke it'. We seem to have significantly fewer inhibitions regarding our personal space when dealing with our house pets and we are able to express our need for physical contact and closeness more freely.

When horses first meet, they exchange information at first solely with their breath. (Photo: Slawik)

As we have seen, horses have very similar rules to ours in their relationships with each other. On first contact, they stretch out their necks in order to keep maximum distance while inhaling each other's breath and thus exchanging information.

We people extend our arms and shake hands in order to keep our distance when meeting for the first time. Horses also only gradually permit reduction of this distance, as long as both parties like each other, for example, by carefully smelling each other's

necks. But it is just as possible at this stage that loud squeals or a kick with the forelegs signal that further contact is unwanted. Horses that are related to each other or know each other well are allowed to enter the personal space unhindered, or else their physical closeness will be regulated by signals so subtle that we will miss them if we do not observe well.

With horses we think it is 'sweet' when they snuggle up closely to us. We often reward them with a treat and thus reinforce this behaviour. However, what this tells the horse on a specifically equine psychological level about the human is that 'you are ranked lower than I am, because you allow me to intrude into your personal space and for this lack of respect you even give me a reward'.

If a horse then becomes insistent and searches our pockets and hands for further treats, the person either moves away (and further emphasises his or her lower rank) or verbally rejects the animal – 'Now that's enough of that, Giacomo/Prince/…!' This reprimand, however, has no real meaning for the horse; it can only tell by the tone of the voice at the most if what was said was meant positively or negatively. I would not be surprised if many horses became desensitised, that is, dulled, by their owner's constant chatter. In addition to the verbal reprimand, some owners might even punish their horses physically in the form of a slap or a blow on the breast. I hope you have realised how little sense this makes to the horse, and what strange creatures we must seem to be in his eyes when we behave in such a manner.

Owners like these often complain about 'dominance problems' and report that their horses 'suddenly and without reason' bite them. But this is nothing more than a logical consequence of our behaviour, because as a lower-ranking individual we are not permitted to enter the personal space of the horse without asking permission, and the horse emphatically reminds us of this by putting back its ears, showing its teeth, biting

or using other aggressive signals or combinations of these (aggressive displays or agonistic behaviour).

Friendly leadership right from the start

It is advisable to consider a few points before approaching a horse for the first time. The greeting should always be friendly, but the degree of determined firmness should vary – just as in everyday life. In

This horse signals clearly to its rider what it thinks of her leadership qualities. (Photo: Slawik)

plain English that is greeting a child quite differently from, say, a high-ranking military officer or an old aunt. Rank and social position are always taken into consideration. In the same way, we have to make a far stronger impression on a young adult stallion than on a six-month-old filly.

What is social behaviour?

Every type of contact, involvement and work with a horse constitutes social interaction. If we develop our knowledge of horses' social behaviour by learning to understand which (communicative) signals and displays (combinations of signals) have what meaning in a particular social context, we will increase our chances of achieving a harmonious partnership.

There is an old saying: 'You will never get a second chance to make a first impression'. That is true for meetings between people as well as between human and horse; often the very first impression counts and is difficult to correct at a later stage. If you want to build up a good relationship with a new horse, you should prepare yourself for the first meeting.

• Approach the horse in a confident manner, holding yourself erect. Remember though that horses rarely walk towards each other directly in a straight line, but rather at an angle and in semi-circular movements because that way the lateral positioning of their eyes gives them a better field of vision and because the approach from the side is a far less aggressive and predator-like gesture.

• By standing slightly sideways you appear more friendly and more inviting than in a frontal pose. It is all right to take up eye contact with the horse, but staring into its eyes is quickly interpreted as aggressive. Eye contact should therefore be established carefully and in moderation.

Friendly and curious first contact between human and horse. (Photo: Slawik)

A position taken up from the side appears more friendly and inviting. (Photo: Slawik)

Letting the horse smell the back of your hand is a good basis for the first contact. (Photo: Wentscher)

• Offer the horse the back of your hand to smell. The horse will gain important information: for example, whether you are frightened. It will definitely remember your smell and recognise you by it later. It cannot identify us by the colour of our 'coat', because we constantly change our clothing. But this does not present a problem to the horse because horses can remember facial features as well as we can, although they re-recognise us predominantly by our silhouette, our posture and our movement. These characteristics will tell the horse quite a lot about us: a person walking upright and purposefully appears stronger, more confident and of higher ranking than someone who seems to be aimless and depressed and who shuffles slowly along. Superior leaders walk with their heads held high, firm of step, and do not appear hesitant or flustered. If we also manage to look fit and happy without any sign of nervousness, every horse will develop interest in us and will react in a positive manner.

• After the horse has smelled your hand, you should enter its personal space and stroke its neck or withers – of course only if you are dealing with a friendly horse.

• A horse that puts its ears back and shows its teeth should not be touched, but you should not move away either. How you approach it depends on your experience and on the information you have been given about the horse. Some horses will indeed bite people, but most will only display this extremely hostile and aggressive behaviour in order to keep people at bay because of their previous negative experiences. Let it be said as a general note: always leave horses alone to eat their hard food. You would not want to be disturbed during your lunch either.

• If the horse is friendly, make a point of being the first to enter the personal space by standing to one side of the horse and stroking or scratching the horse's neck or withers. This conveys to him your friendly and positive attitude and you can consolidate this first companionable bonding in your relationship. Do speak to the horse if you want to, but with care. Speak softly and gently. Horses have excellent hearing. If you feel nervous, try not to speak too much, because the horse will be able to detect the level of your tension in the tone of your voice. By making the first move to establish closer contact, you signal to the horse that you, as the higher-ranked, are taking over the responsibility and that you will therefore be the one to act rather than react. This is a highly important criterion for true leadership.

• You can extend the proper horse-greeting ceremony further by leaning your face against the horse's neck and breathing in its scent. As horses usually smell very good, this should not be difficult for you to do.

Solution methods for aggressive horses

Horses that appear aggressive are often socially insecure. Instead of evaluating such behaviour as negative, it is possible to develop a good relationship with positive leadership. In particular, those very horses that have previously been aggressive often prove to have a golden 'heart' and often become

high achievers as sport comrades once they find an owner whom they can trust.

When meeting an aggressive-looking horse, I first stand still and wait until it has calmed down. I avoid direct eye contact but maintain my position and signal to the horse in this way that I am not to be intimidated. If the horse relaxes, I move away for a moment – but not before it has completely stopped threatening me. A moment later I return to my previous place and wait again until the horse again stops threatening me. Depending on the intensity of the aggressive signals or displays, I can repeat these 'advance and withdraw' tactics several times. The important thing at this stage is to stick to my secure place until the horse relinquishes its aggressive attitude and gestures, and only then do I walk away. In this way I tell the horse, firstly, that I am not afraid and, secondly, that I will remove the tension my presence creates as soon as a 'neutral' atmosphere prevails. It learns that I am not a danger to it.

A person acting as predator would not withdraw from its prey, in this case the horse. The mental structures of horses are limited, and for that reason a person associated with pain or discomfort (for example, someone using a badly fitted saddle to ride with or a rider who bumps about in the saddle and permanently inflicts pain to the horse's sensitive mouth) is automatically registered in the category of 'dangerous predator'. Horses will certainly learn that such dangers are not life-threatening, but they will try to avoid someone causing them permanent pain or distress as much as they will try to avoid a lethal enemy.

Many horses will react with surprise when you move away from them, as they are not familiar with such behaviour from humans. It will arouse their curiosity about you since you behave differently to what they expect. This is now the point at which you offer this previously so aggressive horse the back of your hand to smell.

If you are able now to touch the horse on its withers or neck, you have as good as won. With very scared horses it is advisable to stroke only with the back of your hand, keeping your fingers closed.

Because of their specific mental make-up as flight animals, some horses quite simply

A horse cannot see the area directly between its eyes – touching it there will help to build up trust. (Photo: Wentscher)

feel fear when confronted with humans. It is not always a good idea to put your hand out directly to touch a horse's face. Once it accepts you stroking its neck, you then have the chance to work your way slowly towards the head and finally stroke the area between its eyes. This gentle stroking (but not patting of any kind) is an excellent method of building up trust because the horse cannot see this part of the body itself. Avoid direct eye contact in order to eliminate all trace of aggression.

Solution methods for frightened horses

A scared or timid horse has also had bad experiences, or else its genetic disposition concerning social competence is not fully developed. These horses, too, can be relatively easily reconditioned through positive treatment and success in learning.

Initially you behave in a similar manner to that which you use with an aggressive horse. You approach the horse as closely as it will tolerate without it running away, then you stand still at this place, and only then move away. Again, because your behaviour is not seen as aggressive, the horse will become curious. Because you behave so differently from the predator which after approaching its prey stays by it, this move will awake the horse's trust. Finally, you reduce the distance carefully and gradually and when withdrawing do not move so far away. You will most likely be able to touch the horse's neck after a few minutes. The most important thing is that both when advancing towards the horse and when withdrawing you must always move from the side. A frontal position would appear too aggressive and thus would send it running away.

When dealing with a frightened horse it is especially important not to appear as a predator. (Photo: Wentscher)

Look but don't stare

In our culture it is considered polite to look at each other when saying hello. Should a conversation develop, however, we do not usually continue to look into each other's eyes all the time. Often the person talking looks away, while the one listening fixes his gaze on the speaker. Then the roles are reversed and we establish eye contact now and again, but this eye contact is not kept up for long because to us, just as with horses, such sustained staring appears aggressive and threatening. Thus for a successful relationship with your horse, it is important not to gaze at it for long. It is better just occasionally, 'by the way' as it were, to glance at it when checking its reactions, and only to look it directly in the eye for a matter of seconds, preferably with a loving look. The subtlest changes in your expression will not go unnoticed by the horse that is a master of non-verbal communication.

No food needed: horses can become as good as 'addicted' to gentle stroking and scratching of the neck by way of reward. (Photo: Wentscher)

Greeting with food

Far too many horses are used to being fed treats from their owner's hands. Food constitutes a primary reinforcement for them. This means they do not have to learn that food is something positive (as completely opposed to a pat or slap on the neck, used by many riders as a form of reward, which, however, is completely foreign to a horse and whose positive meaning it must first learn).

I know horses that perform a whole range of the most acrobatic disciplines without even being asked to do so simply because they hope to be rewarded with a treat, and I have to admit that I am not impressed by this behaviour but am, on the contrary,

Foto: Wentscher

55

embarrassed. Horses can be so easily motivated that, unasked, they show a certain pattern of behaviour learnt through the incentive of food, just for the sake of their hoped-for reward. No matter how perfect the performance was, under no circumstances should it be rewarded but, instead, ignored, if you did not expressly ask for it.

On the other hand, I also know many horses today that have become similarly 'addicted' to stroking, patting and scratching or to verbal praise.

For me this is the proof that it is possible to teach horses equally well without using food from the hand as a motivator and that they can learn to appreciate stroking and scratching just as much as the reward of food.

I have always had a problem with worming myself into a horse's favour and 'buying' its sympathy and friendship with treats. I must also say that the behaviour of many a rider, who first improperly maltreats his horse with spurs and crop and then tries to make up for it by feeding it sweets, is dubious if not reprehensible.

For this reason I usually completely avoid feeding horses from the hand and advise every horse owner to weigh up carefully what type of reward to use in what situations.

If you do not want to change the habit because your horse has been used to treats for years and you are afraid that he might send you a written warning should you no longer have an apple for him in your pocket, there are still certain rules to apply. Your

horse should be friendly towards you and not greet you with ears laid back and teeth bared: in such cases there can be no treat. The same applies if your horse shoves you around, pushes against you or steps on your toes. Again it is a fundamental mistake to reward it for this. In the former case, you should wait until the horse looks friendly (horses can be very sweet if they want something…) and in the latter, make the horse step back through short, sharp backward pulls to its head collar. If the horse is not wearing one, you can look it firmly in the eye and snap your fingers on the level of its eyes to send it back. That way you avoid a physical confrontation which a human can easily lose.

Now if your horse is waiting sweetly and patiently and gazes longingly at you with its big, faithful eyes when you come, you can, if you want, feed it a treat, but it must be you who enters the private space first – on no account the other way round. Then it is best always to feed the same amount. If you give your horse a bucket of apples on its birthday and offer only a single carrot the day after, it will have every right on its side to be disappointed. Your horse does not know that it had a birthday party yesterday. But as animals of habit, horses learn quickly that they are going to get one treat and 'that's all'. It is a good idea to use a signal to show that there are no more treats and that neither you nor your clothes are made of 'horse-sweet-paper'. Stretch out your hands, for example, and say 'All gone', and then do not feed it any more. If you do this consistently, your horse will soon understand. Ask the other people in the stable not to hand-feed your horse either; if necessary, attach a polite notice to the box, field or paddock.

If you have a young horse or have acquired a new one, try to discipline yourself not to introduce hand-feeding of treats. It is certainly permitted to place a treat in the food trough, for example, when the horse returns from its field to the stable. And, of course, it is better and far more humane to use a bucket of carrots for a horse that has problems with vets or farriers, or a haynet when it is being transported, rather than restraining it with a twitch or bottles of tranquillisers. However, correct training with the help of professionals is always the best option.

Calming a frightened horse with food is certainly a better option than using a twitch. (Photo: Wentscher)

Leadership
and partnership

In the first part of the book we looked at the way social structures of herds are composed and at alternatives to these. We have seen that horses do indeed live within a form of hierarchy which is, however, far less rigid-ly ordered than previously thought, and in which friendly interactions with regard to ranking are far more common than con-frontations that are hostile. We humans, too, live mostly in family or patchwork family groups, even though we tend today no longer to live with several generations under one roof. These groups are also structured according to a hierarchy in that the legal guardians or parents are primarily those who 'have the say'. As with horses, our rankings are typically established in a friendly rather than a hostile manner. Another big similarity is our need to survive both as individuals and as a species and to pass our genes on to further generations.

Without trying to humanise the horse, it is useful for us to acknowledge the similarities of these social structures (in a friendly hierarchy) in order to develop a harmonious relationship with our horses.

There are some horse-gurus who promise us that by following their techniques we can develop a partnership based on equality with our horses – an idea that appeals directly to us as peace-loving people. At the other end of the scale, there are those riding establishments and instructors that expect permanent, robot-like obedience from the horse, which they do not hesitate to exact with force.

An intelligent, open-minded person, intent on learning, might nowadays well be confused by these extreme and diverse fronts and possibly quite rightly ask whether you should get your horse to learn self-carriage with spa treatment or with telepathy.

Common sense tells us to use our own powers of thought in all controversial issues and not to adopt anybody else's untested opinions or methods uncritically. So you

Are you also your local tack shop's best client? For the horse it does more harm than good. (Photo: Slawik)

should ask yourself: is it at all possible to live in an equal partnership with a horse, and if so, what would this be like? What does it mean for horse and human to develop a partnership, and what can each party gain from it and offer the other? How can a person give his or her best and also bring out 'the best' in the animal, his partner?

Respect, trust, and friendship – all this is possible when we prove to be a wise and positive partner to the horse. (Photo: Wentscher)

If we want our horse to become a willing partner, it is our job to find out how we ourselves can become a positive and supportive friend to our horse – in good as well as in difficult situations.

It is my personal belief that we can work with horses and spend our free time with them in great harmony. Despite the significant intellectual differences and also our position as the decision-maker, a relationship characterised by mutual respect and friendship is both possible and infinitely desirable.

How can we manage to win over a horse to a relationship like this? What do we have to offer that is valuable and of importance to our horse?

It is in a horse's nature to search for companionship which it will happily join and follow if it has found a human whom it can trust completely. This trust will develop through a calm and positive charisma on our part and through the wise, well-thought-out decisions that we humans, as the principle co-ordinators in our mini-group, take for our horse. These include realistic expectations with regard to our common performance abilities – but not a democratic discussion as to whether the horse is allowed to binge on the food supply at night.

Often, particularly in potentially difficult situations, people react to their horse's behaviour like predators, usually without realising or intending to do so. Horses are restrained too much and reined in tightly, overbent, forced into trailers, shouted at and hit, or spurred on with violent force.

Behaviour like this will damage the horse's trust because by acting in this way we neglect the horse's need of protective safety. A horse that is subjected to violent force will develop an increased sense of the need for self-protection. This can create a real danger for people involved, and all positive communication breaks down. The horse sees our supposed claim to dominance as an act of aggression and will lose its trust in us, and as a rule trust is destroyed far more quickly than it can be rebuilt.

It is therefore absolutely essential for us as leaders to learn how to apply different active strategies in our desire to achieve our goals.

> *Horses learn what to fear and what not just as well from other horses and people as from themselves.*
>
> *Anonymous*

Violence destroys trust! (Photo: Slawik)

Realistic 'partnership' and friendship with horses

For me partnership with a horse means I never assume that a horse does anything, or refuses to do anything, out of malicious intent or that it deliberately wants to annoy or frustrate me. Partnership also means that the horse and I always act as a team and not as two beings that (constantly) fight against each other. My opinion is that there are very few horses (the few exceptions prove the rule) that shy at 'ghosts' just for fun, although unfortunately many riders believe just that and therefore feel justified in 'belting him one'.

I once came across a horse that went lame each time the rider approached it with the saddle. Unlike the owner, I was thrilled by the creative intelligence of this horse, and secretly wished more horses could be so smart. Try to imagine what this horse must have gone through before it learned to escape work with its rider by hobbling.

The owner was annoyed at all the veterinary bills this horse had caused him without a definite diagnosis ever being produced, instead of acknowledging his horse's intelligence and analysing his own behaviour, tack and all his riding methods in order to find the real reason for the horse's behaviour.

The goal that I have set for myself is that my horses would all choose me as their owner and that all those horses that attend my courses, including those in training, would also always choose me to be their favourite trainer.

When kept in conditions like these, horses become depressed (Photo: Slawik)

In order to become the perfect partner for your horse, first analyse your stable management regime. A diet suited to performance requirements, fresh water access at all times, social contacts, freedom of movement and the absence of pain or stress are all essential for its mental and physical well-being.

Because of its natural instincts still being fully intact and because of its genetic make-up, a suffering or injured horse will suffer silently, because in the wild an injured animal is an easy prey for predators. That is why horses hide their pain as much as possible and throughout their evolutionary history have not developed any specific pain vocalisations. Hence, just because you fail to register any sounds indicating pain from your horse does not necessarily mean that it is well and happy!

Fear and stress also compromise your horse's health. Whole books could be written on the subject – but there are a few points that I very much want to draw your attention to. I was recently working one of my horses in training in a 'perfectly normal' indoor riding school and was witness involuntarily to various forms of horse torture. From a fellow rider's horse came numerous grunting sounds (relatively tone-free, perhaps similar to the grunt some tennis players produce on service) – within one hour I heard it nine times. It is probably the only sound horses make when they are in pain. I have had to bear several situations like this in my time for I know that most riders do not take kindly to being told or advised what to do. Each of us is at a

For some people, treating horses cruelly has become so 'normal' that they cannot possibly imagine how fulfilling a partnership could actually be. (Photo: Slawik)

High-level dressage is perfectly possible without the use of whip and spurs. (Photo: Wentscher)

different learning stage, a fact which should be respected, and we all deserve individual help. In many cases it is sufficient to set a good example. Some people have not even suspected the very idea that the way they handle their horse is unfulfilling and frustrating.

I like to avoid the use of spurs or whip in order to demonstrate that one can certainly ride successfully without these aids – but not because I disapprove of their use comprehensively. In my opinion, however, it is not legitimate to desensitise a horse to them through incorrect use and then justify applying them even more because the horse appears lazy. Therefore I sometimes have to fight against my own resigned frustration and ask myself if it is really possible to enjoy riding while the horse under the saddle grunts with pain? Horses do not need to be beaten to make them walk into a trailer, dark box or solarium, and bald patches or jab wounds in their flanks are not an indication of the correct use of spurs either.

We do not live in a perfect world, but by setting a good example we can try to improve it a little. Do not invest in a trainer who exercises violence in order to write up successes; and if you train horses yourself, try not to repeat the mistakes that, for thousands of years, generations before us and with us have made. Encourage your client mentally and physically to take an active part in the process and refuse to take on horses to be 'patched up' without teaching the owners themselves to improve their horsemanship.

Am I the owner that my horse would choose for himself?

We can learn a lot about ourselves from horses, because their reactions to our behaviour are honest and upright. You cannot impress a horse with an annual salary of $500.000 or by having won a Miss World competition. The only things that count are our personality and our ability to communicate (non-verbally). Physical fitness as well, plus a feeling for realistic expectations as to what we can achieve, friendliness and creativity –these are the things we convey to our horses and which are then mirrored in their behaviour. (More about this on page 106.)

Horses as herd and flight animals also learn by imitating the behaviour of a social partner, that is, through received vibes and behavioural patterns, and these 'role models' can be other horses as well as people. The first role model in a horse's life is its mother, the mare from whom it learns social competence and well-tested action strategies. Later in life other horses become influential, too, and also, in those cases where a close bond has developed, people. When the human social partner is able to convey his feelings (vibes) successfully to the horse, his behaviour becomes a model for the (later) behaviour of the horse, together with the emotions connected with it.

Your personal charisma plays a large part in the role assigned you by a horse. (Photo: Slawik)

Being what I want to be

Before we turn back to discussing horses, we should pause for a moment just to think about ourselves and try by exploring our own psyche to examine how we appear to others and what attributes best describe us as we are now. One's basic character is relatively stable, whereas behaviour, behavioural patterns, physical fitness, mood and spirit can change. The following characteristics are helpful in enabling us to understand ourselves:

Optimistic	– Pessimistic
Consistent	– Inconsistent
Focused	– Inattentive, chaotic
Self-confident	– Unsure of oneself
Brave	– Scared
Independent	– Dependent
Physically fit	– Physically unfit
Mentally balanced	– Moody
Motivated	– Unmotivated
Calm	– Hectic
Patient	– Impatient
Active	– Passive
Friendly	– Unfriendly
Responsible	– Irresponsible
Relaxed	– Tense
Disciplined	– Undisciplined
Critical	– Uncritical
Flexible	– Rigid
Playful	– Reserved

Be honest with yourself, and identify your weaknesses in order to turn them into strengths. Do not trust an inner voice that is unkind to you, but be brave enough to acknowledge your weaker points. Stay objective, positive and forgiving, as good trainers and leaders should be. Think also about how your horse would describe you if it had the intellectual ability to do so.

I myself am a very impatient person and I used to get terribly flustered when something did not work out immediately. Therefore, I was deliberately exposed to specific situations that would try my patience to the extreme in order to teach me how important patience is. Be prepared when the time comes for you to meet your teacher!

My teachers appeared during a long tour I made of the USA. I was working on a big farm importing mustangs from Nevada to California in order to tame them there and break them in. It was not just new to me that I had to tame a horse first before I could train it. I was also faced with the fact that of the fifteen horses under my care, three had had head collars put on them at some earlier point in their lives which, with time, had become too small, had rubbed the skin on their heads raw and had grown into the flesh. Removing them by cutting them free was a painful process. For this ghastly ordeal, the mustangs were confined in a very small pen so that they could hardly move or escape; otherwise without tranquillisers this procedure would not have been possible.

The horses were kept in adjacent paddocks about 90 square feet in size. It was no great problem after a while to get close to them and touch them, but never would they allow me to get anywhere near their heads. So there I was, all by myself, in the scorching Californian heat, with three horses that never ever for the rest of their lives wanted to wear a head collar again, let alone a bridle, and with my 'Come on, it's got to work now' mentality I was not getting any further. There was no trick either that would work. You can't bribe horses with treats, carrots or apples if they do not know what they are.

I was able to touch the three of them and groom them, pick up their feet and brush their tails, but as soon as I approached with anything looking remotely like a head collar, they refused to let me get anywhere near them. I was close to tears with frustration. I then hung the head collars in the paddocks next to the place where the hay was given them so as to let the horses see them every day. A head collar without a person did not seem to bother them at all. In the end I managed it – but only because I was focused, calm and precise and in many a lengthy sequence approached them with the halters hanging over my arm while I practised the 'advance and withdraw' method. Later, when I was able to touch the horses with the halter now in my hand, I would stroke them generously and in this way remove their fear of physical contact. These horses had been wild at some point in the past before they were driven together and caught to be taken to one of the big mustang transit farms in the

USA. They had no reason to accept that wearing a head collar could become a meaningful part of their lives, especially since these objects had caused them such horrific pain before.

The mustangs never fought me directly, but they were very fast and agile and could easily get away. So it was a big challenge to my patience, and I only very gradually realised that I was achieving nothing and simply making the situation worse for myself when I allowed anger, resignation and frustration to rise, just because I could not progress in the conventional way my books on the subject had taught me. There was only one really practical solution to the problem: I had to completely 'reformat' myself, or rather, my thinking structures, and learn to see everything that I experienced there as nothing other than positive and enriching to my life. I had to work hard on myself and profited immensely from the experience. What I actively learnt was that feelings such as impatience, fury and personal disappointment have absolutely no place in the intelligent and successful training of horses.

With the necessary amount of self-discipline, goodwill and a raised frustration threshold, you will not only achieve good results with horses but you will also acquire important and positive qualities of character for yourself. A solution-orientated and strategic approach as well as a careful analysis of where you are now and where you want to go will help you to develop and realise your individual plan of action. You need to note positive changes and reward any intermediate success promptly and appropriately.

To put it in a nutshell: the more disciplined you are with yourself during your training regime and in your relationship with your horse, the greater your successes will be.

Genuine authority: the key to harmony

'He who speaks the truth should always keep a saddled horse at the ready.'

Armenian saying

With all the tips and tricks and methods that diverse 'horse whisperers' use, often nothing more is involved than rules to be learnt and put into practice with which to make it clear to the horse that the human is the higher-ranking being. The purchase of certain articles or devices for training has also shown itself to be a popular way of curing 'problem horses' of their trouble spots.

Methods and devices can only be as good or as helpful as the person who uses, masters or interprets them. Apart from the learning of techniques, developing your own personality as a trustworthy and competent leader is the most important factor in achieving success. It's a good idea to find another successful horse person to act as role model whose methods at first you try to copy as well as possible.

The sporadic attempt to dominate your horse only in certain circumstances will not necessarily improve your relationship seriously in the long run. This is because horses sense so accurately whether we are only 'acting' authority when exercising certain practices or whether we really do have the authentic authority and foresight required for dealing with a sensitive flight animal.

A certain technique or aid can therefore only be used as a means of support but will not in itself alone achieve any concrete results or any real improvement in a difficult situation.

It is similarly problematic if you try to use certain exercises to impress on your horse that you have a higher ranking but then fail to fulfil your role as a truly responsible leader in every other situation that occurs. This will only confuse the horse and prevent the development of a trusting relationship between you both. Horses, like humans, do not want to be suppressed. However, they are far happier, more co-operative when working and less stressed if they can follow someone they trust.

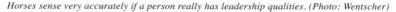

Horses sense very accurately if a person really has leadership qualities. (Photo: Wentscher)

Horses (subconsciously) long for leadership – but that is a very different thing from submission. In a material world full of objects that make no sense to a horse, a human radiating calm, strength and security can be an assuring source of orientation. Thus a horse will continue to 'test' this person until it can completely trust him; this is the horse's life-saving instinct. The problems involved in the question of ranking arise on the one hand from the strong instincts of the horse and on the other from people's inconsistency and disregard of the idea of leadership.

The horse only needs to know that it can trust its rider, that this rider will know how to avoid situations causing it pain or distress, and that it can put its full confidence in him to make the right decisions for its survival.

Horses in a herd will trust an older animal that due to its age has sufficient experience to decide whether the group needs to flee or not. Rankings in a herd are for this reason always intact and at the same time sound, because daughters or high-ranking companions of the leading mare take over her place as leader if she becomes too old to be able to lead the herd. An injured horse will not lead a herd either. Because of the fact that within the complex of the herd constellation there are always other high-ranking horses that can take over the leadership, the safety of the herd is assured.

Thus the other members of the herd fol-

A horse will only trust those people who protect it from pain. (Photo: Slawik)

low their leaders because they trust them to make the right decisions to secure their survival and not primarily because they are dominated by them. The privilege of dominance in this case follows not from the state or process itself but from exercising the responsibility of the position that an individual has assumed.

If we truly love horses for what they are, we have to accept that they constantly try to assess whether they can trust us – whether we prove ourselves to be trustworthy or not. From this arises the simple rule:

A horse does not act with malicious intent: its survival instincts dictate that it must test a person's trustworthiness. (Photo: Slawik)

The horse is given information as to whether a person is suited as a leader by a whole range of factors – from body posture to skin conductance. (Photo: Wentscher)

the less consistent we are in all questions of responsibility, the more they have to test us – not because of malicious intent but because their instincts prevent them from acting any differently.

That has yet another consequence. I have to be able to react competently in every situation that arises if I expect 100% trust and co-operation from my horse. People who do not work with horses all day long often do not find it easy to see the world with its potential dangers through the eyes (and the other highly developed senses) of a horse.

It takes practice and the basic willingness to become more of a proper horse person than one has been as yet. However, rankings are not established in the actual moment of imminent danger – it all happens a lot earlier. At the very first moment of contact, you will have given your horse a huge amount of information about your qualities as leader through your unique posture, smell, muscle tone and skin conductance, through your voice, your body movements and through your inner calm. Your horse will react to you accordingly.

Theories of equine communication

The senses of horses are far more developed than ours, and so horses gain a lot of information about us and our wel-lbeing of which we ourselves are completely unaware and which we therefore do not take into consideration in our dealings with them. Thus we 'train' our horse all the time we are together by unwittingly, unconsciously, sending non-verbal signals, signs and gestures with our bodies. With every piece of information, with each and every action and reaction to the horse's behaviour on our part, we tell the horse whether we are suited as leaders. That is why it is not enough just to make a few attempts at establishing a hierarchy through certain exercises or with the use of certain aids, because dominance is not a permanent status that is confirmed at some point once and for all and then automatically remains 'til the end of time.

Furthermore, it is not characteristic of higher-ranked individuals to force the lower-ranked to behave in a certain way. A leading mare does not force the other members of the herd to follow her. Within the herd it is more a case of communicating to lower-ranked social partners what they should not do. Obedience is not a reliable indicator for status within the hierarchy, because communication problems can also be a reason for disobedience.

It is possible for a horse to be extremely obedient and friendly and to give the impression that a hierarchy has been established in its owner's favour, yet not to accept this owner as a competent leader. (Photo: Wentscher)

The horse will (quite rightly) check us carefully until it is certain that we are responsible leaders. This process can last for the entire time we spend with the horse. Once the animal is convinced, however, that we are competent leaders, the tests become less frequent, are drastically reduced or, with time, possibly stop altogether. In some instances it is even possible in certain situations for us to present ourselves partially as lower-ranked (for example, the horse is allowed to rub its head against us), but at decisive moments it still does not question our leadership.

Depending on the character and previous experience a horse has had, this testing of our ranking can drive the owner almost crazy. It is far more sensible to give your full thought to the whole issue and systematically to search for a solution as to how to deal with it, instead of permanently fighting, thinking badly of the animal or even labelling it a 'problem horse'.

Take the following example: you want to collect your horse from the field but it tears itself away and runs back to its companions.

From this you can, for example, deduce that:

• Your horse has learned not to take you very seriously as a leader.

• Your horse prefers to eat luscious green grass than to work with you, running round and round in the indoor riding school

• You have acted in such a way that you have (unwittingly) driven your horse away from you.

• Your horse could not stay with you because you yourself were so tense and scared that it suspected some kind of danger lurking.

• Your horse in general enjoys neither your company nor working with you.

• Your horse has had neither a proper upbringing nor training.

• Your horse just does not like the company of humans.

This list could be continued at length.

So the next time that you take up the bridle and whip as 'weapons' and make rigorous use of both without understanding the horse's behaviour, you will indeed be demonstrating to your horse that you can cause it pain or distress but not, however, that you are working it with responsibility and as its friend. The horse, of course, learns to expect painful consequences for its behaviour that are connected to a particular person, but it does not learn to follow you trustfully and to stay with you because you are the leader in this herd of two.

If instead of this you energetically decide to carry out a polished piece of dominance training with your horse and with certain exercises try to convince it that you claim to be the leader, your horse will only learn that you have managed with mechanical means to get it to perform certain movements in a certain place and in a certain situation, all of which will certainly help you in your claim to leadership, but it still will not accept you as the responsible partner with whom it likes to be.

And yet these are the well-meaning tips and pieces of advice that your riding instructor or riding friends will give you when problems of this sort crop up – and that with a clear conscience. Unfortunately, tips of this kind often result in a horse only appearing to be more obedient because it wants to avoid pain, but not in an improvement in the quality of its relationship with you. Submission is not necessarily a true indicator for an established hierarchy or for good leadership.

Competence in communication and intelligent handling of a horse takes more than just the use of a few devices inducing obedience; it requires us to become personally involved in the whole process of schooling. Therefore, instead of 'arming' yourself with countless aids and labelling the horse a 'problem horse' (have you ever wondered where the stud farm for the breed 'problem horse' is and what strange pedigree is produced there?), you should ask yourself honestly whether what you intend to do makes sense or not and whether it can be successful. Dare to make a realistic assessment of your own skills with horses which automatically involve your degree of communicative competence and ability to act accordingly – this can save your life.

If you do not create the impression of having authentic authority and your horse is not one of the more experienced or unshakable representatives of the species, try to find competent help and deliberately collect positive experiences aimed at boosting your self-confidence and restoring your trust in horses.

Defining your own leadership style

The relationship with your horse gives you important information about the effect and also effectiveness of your body language and charisma. Particularly when encountering repeated difficulties, you need to check if you are reacting with an adequate measure of authority and whether you are using reprimands or praise at the right time.

If you are by nature a timid and frightened person and your horse is young and very challenging, you have to work hard on yourself at establishing a clear hierarchy. The more horse and human are suited to each other, the better are the chances for successful and harmonious teamwork. Therefore, before buying a horse you should definitely pause to give your leadership qualities a thought and try to define your own leadership style. Even if you have already found a horse – or it has found you – it is worth subjecting yourself to critical though amicable self-analysis. Your horse will definitely reveal to you whether the picture you have of yourself reflects the picture it has of you.

A person with repeated and apparently inexplicable leadership problems can with self-analysis find his way to the root of the conflict. Maybe your expectations are not reflected by your body language. Or is your leadership style perhaps aimed at companionship and tolerance, whereas your horse requires a certain measure of fair authority to compensate for your giving him too little

What is going wrong here? Precise and critical self-analysis will provide better solutions than just blaming the horse. (Photo: Slawik)

orientation? Or are you exceedingly dominant but failing to give clear signals, so that confusion is created instead of obedience?

Establishing rankings

As we have seen, via body language, voice, smell, muscle and skin tone we give the horse a lot of information which it analyses in order to establish a ranking. This instinctive behaviour is anchored in its genes to secure its survival.

A higher-ranking horse (in the herd) initiates and concludes social interactions, and it is the first to enter the personal space of others. It is therefore useful for us to apply the very same principles that horses use among each other to our own interaction with them. Highly ranked horses control resources and have access to them whenever they want. We humans, too, control many of our horse's resources, determine his daily schedule, and in this way gain a certain advantage with regard to status.

A hierarchy is also established through imposing postures which when intensified contain elements of aggressive (or threatening) behaviour. But demonstrating imposing behaviour alone, even with moderate to increasingly aggressive signals and displays, is not enough in itself to establish a hierarchy.

The addressee has to acknowledge this, either with his own signals of submission or with retreat or, alternatively, he must vigorously threaten or send imposing signals in return until it is quite clear who will take over leadership. If, now, we ourselves want to establish the question of leadership with our horse 'positively', we must preferably use those very modes of behaviour which contribute to creating friendliness in our relationship.

Examples of these are: who can move towards whom (without the horse having to withdraw)? Who protects whom from attacks from other herd members? Who initiates mutual grooming with whom (allogrooming)?

Imposing gestures can also include aggressive signals; a social partner has either to acknowledge or reject them. (Photo: Slawik)

Attention and self-awareness

> *'The world is not threatened by evil people, but by those who allow evil to take place.'*
>
> *Albert Einstein*

Whether you have problems with your horse or not, it is always of great interest to spend time observing yourself in order to discern how you 'behave' both in the stables and towards your horse and to contemplate on how your horse perceives this behaviour of yours.

Assess the way in which you approach your horse:

• Are you the type that 'drags' himself off to the yard, or are you able to leave all your ailments and personal problems behind as soon as you enter the stables and focus solely on the time you will now spend together with your horse?

• Do you haul your horse out of the stable, or do you greet it in a warm, friendly voice and wait until it moves towards you so that you can then scratch its withers pleasurably until you begin to think about the work you will do together?

• Do you leave your horse tied up for ages while chatting to friends and gesticulating wildly in the stable passageway and then expect it to follow your every verbal command (especially when given in complete sentences) devotedly and without hesitation?

• If your horse starts to paw the ground, do you consider whether it needs to urinate and does not want to do it in the stable passageway? Or do you throw a brush at it and several threats as well?

• Are you one of those people who take it as an insult when your horse shifts its weight and, although tied up, moves one step forward to find a more comfortable position?

• Do you tug at the horse's legs regardless of the way it is standing and get angry if it does not lift the hoof immediately for it to be picked out?

• Do you expect your horse after 23 hours locked up in a stable to stand as still as a statue while you bandage all four legs but then twenty minutes later to perform a movement in extended trot fit for Grand Prix?

• Are you secretly convinced that your horse has signed a contract agreeing to having its legs hosed down with cold water or to being squashed into a narrow trailer without knowing what to expect at the end of the journey?

• Did that contract also include paragraphs ruling that the horse may never be allowed to make a mistake and may never be frightened, no matter how confusingly you behave and how strange your demands may seem?

• Do you expect your horse always to be fully motivated, although you would rather lie on the sofa yourself? Do you expect it to perform a perfect piaffe with extravagance or jump the highest oxer only because your friend's horse can do it?

• Do you think your horse could show a little more gratitude because you have spent a fortune on a new stable rug with tendon boots in matching colours?

It is your task to learn how to see the world through your horse's eyes, judging and constantly asking yourself how you can ensure that your horse can fulfil the tasks you set it and demands you make on it without coming into conflict with its instincts.

The importance of body language

Recently I spent some time watching a woman riding her horse, all the while speaking to it in a gentle, friendly voice. At the end of her riding session, she walked off briskly to one side so as to fetch a hoof pick, telling her horse to 'stand'. The horse, to whom clearly defined body language means far more than a thousand words, obediently followed its owner. At that, she abruptly spun round, reviled the horse and tugged at the reins brutishly until it stood once more in its original place. The horse was greatly confused by all this. And again, when she left it a second time it obediently walked after her. Once more it was shouted at and brutally shoved back to its place. The woman's fury escalated and the horse became more and more confused. The worst thing about it was that the woman took this alleged lapse on the part of her horse personally, as though the horse intended to annoy her and deliberately disregard her verbal commands.

When analysing this episode, we can draw three conclusions. Firstly: it is fine to like speaking to your horse as long as you do not expect verbal commands, given 'suddenly' in the midst of the general flow, to be obeyed. How can a horse filter single commands to be obeyed out of all that talk? There are some horses that do seem to react well to spoken commands, for example, when on the lunge, but in my opinion only because the person usually, quite unconsciously, gives minute, physical signals at the same time (let alone the big 'loud' gestures like lifting the whip).

Always ask yourself whether your horse has in fact understood or was able to understand your commands, especially when something goes wrong. If your horse does not follow your command, it will hardly ever be because it comes from 'Problem Town', but far more likely because you have not expressed yourself clearly. Avoid resorting to louder and louder repetitions of the same command, but think out a way instead in which you could communicate your wishes differently.

If you want to teach your horse when it is to stand still and where, first practise 'ground tying' or standing still, for example, by putting the lunge rein on the ground. You should use body language to support this, that is, you do not move away from your horse by turning round but, instead, remain facing it, keeping up eye contact, and moving slowly backwards.

Your horse will understand this much better and willingly obey. This exercise, however, needs to be practised frequently and in different circumstances and places for it to work well and reliably. For safety reasons, however, never leave your horse completely unattended.

Secondly, always remain objective. Insinuating that your horse deliberately disregards or misinterprets your commands is an attitude that will only lead to an impasse and create frustration on both sides. Check your general approach: do you often feel this way 'in real life' and give others the blame? Revise this victim mentality so that you free yourself from it by consciously depriving others of the power to be the reason for your personal misfortunes and failures. Learn in small, well-

organised steps to assume responsibility for your own actions, and reward yourself generously for each positive result.

Constant punishment and rebuke will cloud the relationship between horse and human. It is my impression that many people see the way they train their horse as a wonderful opportunity for demonstrating their alleged strictness and authority in public.

In other words, they shout and tug, jabbing with their spurs and hitting away with their whips, in order to show all the other riders and owners how competently they know how to deal with their horse and that they never let their horse 'get away with anything'. Should it be the case that you have conducted a

'Look how strict I am!' If you need this image, you had better choose a different sport. (Photo: Slawik)

friendly but honest self-analysis and recognised yourself in this portrayal, make a conscious decision as to what is more important to you, your reputation as a 'tough trainer always with the upper hand' or, alternatively, as a rider with a harmonious relationship to his horse, and then adjust your actions accordingly. Remember also to take seriously your duty to set a good example to children and young riders.

'If you cannot be a good example, then at least be a good example of what not to be.'

Anonymous

Bucking can be a displacement activity if the horse is subjected to a painful situation that reminds it of previous painful experiences. (Photo: Slawik)

Consider whether what you expect from your horse is realistic. Most things that we do with our horses or that they do for us make very little sense to them or even go completely against their nature. However, they are very adaptable and good at learning and usually play along. But this should not lead us to believe that they always understand what is expected of them. It goes against a horse's nature to stand still somewhere on its own. As a flight animal it is constantly on the move and as a highly social animal it does not like to be on its own. Imagine how you would feel if you had to wait half an hour at a bus stop, quite alone and with darkness falling (and no mobile

phone). At least you know that the bus will arrive at some point. A horse, living for the moment, living entirely in the present, might feel punished or at least feel very uneasy to be left alone because, unlike us, it does not know how long this situation is going to last.

And in conclusion, thirdly; if it so happens that you really (justifiably) do have to discipline your horse, do not prolong the angry situation. It is better to ask the horse to perform a small, easy task in exactly the same place and then to reward the horse honestly and generously for its obedience. Horses relate very well to a context and will avoid places where they once experienced pain. If forced to return to such places, they can become so unwilling and tense that they have no choice but to release this tension with displacement activities (shying followed by flight, rearing or bucking).

If your horse is primarily conditioned by receiving rewards, the omission of such can be punishment enough. A horse should only be disciplined seriously if, for example, it violates your personal space or if, as a young horse, it challenges your rules and tolerance limits. Both constitute a violation of the ranking and a short, clear and unemotional punishment should follow. Immediately afterwards, you should create a positive atmosphere and resume normal, concentrated work. Horses certainly remember negative experiences but that is something very different from holding grudges. Set your horse a good example and re-establish a positive environment as soon as possible.

Becoming friends

In order to become a friend and valued companion to your horse, you should first find out what your horse likes. Most domesticated horses enjoy being groomed, scratched and stroked. Horses that are friends mutually groom each other and through the invasion of each other's private space strengthen their bond. I often stroke a particularly difficult horse along the dock or take the time to comb out its tail carefully with my fingers (toddering the tail) – this enables horses to let themselves relax beautifully and to associate the human with a positive experience.

Contrary to common belief and practice, horses do not like firm slaps on the neck or other body parts. Horses are as sensitive all over their bodies as we are at our fingertips and therefore prefer to be touched gently. Slapping the neck is a so-called 'secondary positive enforcement', that is, the horse must first learn that this gesture is intended as something positive, whereas 'primary positive enforcement' like easing pressure, pauses during a work session, grooming and food, will be understood as a reward immediately, without the need of any learning process.

Relaxing breaks are a suitable reward for every horse. (Photo: Wentscher)

It is most likely due to an adaptation to domestication that most horses enjoy being talked to in a calm and loving voice. When doing so you should reduce your words to just a few, speaking quietly, because horses hear much better than we do.

If the occasion arises that you do have to discipline a horse, an angry facial expression or a sharp 'No' with a sensitive horse are enough. The horse will easily sense the difference to your usually neutral or friendly expression and your soft, gentle voice.

Be calm, relaxed and friendly when with your horse and teach yourself not to take out your own problems on the horse. If you notice that on one day you feel particularly anxious or tense, do not provoke an argument since your horse will know that something is wrong with you. Turn it out instead of riding, go for a walk together or let it do loose jumping along a jumping lane or, alternatively, you could go out on a slow, easy hack – it would be so much better for both of you, rather than enduring a thoroughly dissatisfying riding lesson.

Be fair to your horse. Horses have a strong sense of justice and know when they have been unfairly treated. Never punish a horse for something that has not immediately happened (up to three seconds!) beforehand. Horses live for the moment – even though they usually remember a lot. If your horse has torn its brand new rug to bits, you must on no account get furious with it later. You will not be awarded the Nobel Peace Prize

A relaxing hack is often better for horse and rider's nerves than a riding lesson begun in a bad mood. (Photo: Wentscher)

for it but it will save you from having a horse that is afraid of you because it sees you as someone who will 'suddenly and for no reason explode'.

Pay attention to what your horse likes and thoroughly dislikes. Many horse owners think they are bad horse people if they do not constantly hose down their horses' legs. Many yards have no warm water. Do not make yourself unpopular by subjecting your horse to this treatment without thought. If it has already 'told' you by dancing around and shying that it hates going to the washing area but you continue to insist, then at least make the procedure as pleasant as possible. Start with the right hind hoof, the one furthest away from the heart, and slowly work your way from the hoof upwards to the hock. This is followed by the left hindleg and right foreleg. Finally let the water run over the left foreleg. Just think how long you would stay together with your partner if he welcomed you every time with an ice-cold shower, no matter how strongly you objected – especially if he shouted at you and forced you to stand still.

Doing something just because all the others do it, and have always done it, is, in my opinion, the worst possible argument with which to explain your action. Here is another example to illustrate this: most people always mount their horses from the left, and most horses are used to it. It stems from the Prussian army regulations of 1871 when the mounted soldiers wore a sword on their left which would have been in the way had they mounted from the right.

Water can be fun as long as you know how to turn it into a positive experience. (Photo: Wentscher)

I am amazed at how many people for this reason sit askew on their horses owing to the considerable variation in the length of their stirrups. This is due to the fact that they always mount from the left, thus putting a heavy strain on the left stirrup, and forget to swap the stirrup leathers regularly to keep them equal. We also know today that the one-sided strain of the weight of a rider mounting from the left, year after year, has a negative effect on the back of the horse (apart from which, the saddle loses its shape). It is therefore best to use a mounting block which nowadays, fortunately, has become popular in more and more stables. Nevertheless, it is still a good idea to learn to mount your horse from the right safely and smoothly, and to accustom your horse to this.

Are you one of those riders whose hands are not (yet) independent of your seat and who therefore provoke a constant chafing in your horse's mouth? If you are not sure, ask someone to observe or film you. Do not be ashamed if it turns out that you are – you are definitely not alone in this. Take a few riding lessons on the lunge with an experienced instructor until your seat has improved, and use a bitless bridle. How can your horse possibly develop a feeling of friendship for you if you have become the personification of pain?

The following list will give you additional ideas as to how you can permanently improve your relationship with your horse.

Greeting

Always be sure to take your time, scratch your horse on the withers and murmur a few friendly words.

Grooming

Horses that are friends enjoy grooming each other. Observe your horse to find out what it likes. Some horses are very sensitive or ticklish – in such cases gentle circular massages with a soft curry-comb made of synthetic materials are helpful. Every horse will relax when the bottom part of its tail is gently and carefully combed or toddered. All horses like to have their necks scratched and stroked – a definite sign of love on your part!

Picking out the hooves

Make sure your horse is standing in the right position in order to be able to give you the required foot. If not, allow it to position itself better or push it gently in the right direction. Softly run your fingers down the leg, which in most cases will be sufficient for the horse to lift it. Tugging at the feathers or the fetlock must be avoided by all means; it only creates resistance – as does everything else that causes pain or discomfort.

Tacking up

An ice-cold bit in winter is certainly no pleasant experience for the horse. Not only 'sensitive' horses prefer the bit to be warmed before they take it, and this will prevent the emergence of a possible problem with tak-

Am example of a bitless bridle. (Photo: Wentscher)

ing the bit in general. Check the bit for sharp edges and replace it if it is worn. People still tend to use very thick bits that are too large for the relatively small mouth of a horse. These can create problems, such as the tongue hanging out. Perhaps you would ride just as well with a bitless bridle like.

Taking off the bridle

Always wait until the horse lets go of the bit itself and do not tug it out of the sensitive mouth or across the teeth.

Saddling

Saddle rugs should never be used if they are full of hair or encrusted with dirt, so as to avoid pressure sores and subsequent (understandable) resistance on the part of the horse. Lambswool rugs and girth sleeves, as well, get very dirty and need careful, regular cleaning. Fat horses in particular, young horses or those whose girths do not fit well often have small rub marks that hurt. Put the saddle (of course, perfectly fitted by an expert) gently on your horse's back and pull the girth up carefully, always in several stages. Unfortunately, there is still

no horses' trade union to take action against badly fitting saddles!

Riding

Take the time to allow your horse the appropriate warming-up and relaxation phases. Make sure that it is physically and mentally fit for the tasks ahead. Should your horse not perform as desired, make a point of asking yourself constantly whether your 'request' has, in fact, been correctly given. Include plenty of relaxing phases (especially after well-performed tasks) and, using long reins, let it stretch its neck and back rather than waiting until it pulls the reins out of your hands in order to tell you that its neck muscles hurt or that it needs a few moments of relaxation before it continues work on raising the forehand. And do take the courage to

Threatening behaviour when the saddle is put on is very often due to the saddle being badly fitted. (Photo: Wentscher)

If the bit is sharp enough, every horse will stay in the enforced position, no matter how much the neck muscles hurt. (Photo: Wentscher)

leave the indoor school now and then. A hack together with friends is one of the most satisfying experiences that there are, particularly if you help and look after each other.

Whip and spurs

The whip and spurs are aids in fine communication only, and should be used sparingly and only for this purpose. They do not belong in unsteady hands or on unstable legs. Use them as little as possible. If you cannot manage that, try to find out what relaxation techniques (autogenic training, yoga and other such methods) could help you. This is a way of actively preventing your horse from becoming desensitised to these aids and dulled, and subsequently, due to its acquired sense of helplessness, from developing a heightened degree of physical pain tolerance.

Riding as a strength-building exercise – that is no fun for the horse and makes it 'sour'. (Photo: Wentscher)

Never forget that a horse has no real means of vocalising its pain, so it is imperative for you to study its non-verbal communication very closely. Some of these signs are switching the tail, pawing the ground, stomping the feet and sweating, as well as resistance to the saddle and girth.

Personal space

As we have seen, maintaining personal space is an important criterion in ranking. In the herd, suckling foals are permitted to enter their mothers' personal space without 'asking'. Stallions are also allowed to come close during the courtship phase and the ensuing covering of the mares because they have courted the mare sufficiently beforehand and have been encouraged by the mare with appropriate optical and olfactory signals. Horses that are friends have usually established a finely defined hierarchy amongst themselves that permits them to enter each other's space in a way so subtle as to be hardly conspicuous to our eyes.

For us, this means that we should be able to enter the personal or protection space of the horse at any time we like and, of course, walk into the stable, paddock or field whenever we want. The horse, however, is never to enter our own personal space without permission. It is possible for a higher-ranked horse to allow a lower-ranked one to enter its space, but it will never under any circumstances draw back or back away with even the slightest movement. It stands (on) its ground, like an unshakable fortress. You must behave in exactly the same manner when you establish your ranking and intend to maintain it. This is especially true if you have problems with your horse and in the past failed to pay any attention to this highly sensitive subject.

In practical terms, this means: tell your horse very clearly but in a friendly way that

Friendly but firm: 'I don't intend to be pushed aside!' (Photo: Wentscher)

it has to give way to you, and not the other way round. Signs of ignoring your personal space are, for example, when the horse steps on your toes, pushes against you or pushes you aside, searches you or your pockets for treats, bangs its head painfully against yours, or generally disregards your personal space by walking straight into or over you.

Some horses even squash their owners with their hindquarters against a wall or to one side – that, too, is an expression of their understanding of his rank.

You must, however, remember in all this that horses permanently kept in a stable without being able to practise social skills with other horses often tend to ignore the 'rules'. This is partly because the only 'contact' these horses have with others is when they are ridden in a school and 'forced' to enter and disregard other horses' personal space. When many riders are working their horses together in the indoor school or in some other small arena, they thereby subject their horses constantly to specific close encounters that in the wild they would never have.

If you want to train your horse not to enter your personal space in future without your express permission, you need to conduct a thorough analysis of your behaviour so far and to plan your future encounters carefully. In order to carry out your concepts successfully, it is imperative to teach your horse that you are the higher-ranked individual and to make it clear when and where and how it has to give way to you. You will succeed in this best if you adopt a new attitude based on your freshly gained knowledge, carefully carried out groundwork and by applying these new principles in all your everyday contact with the horse.

No matter what type of head collar you prefer, it is important that you get yourself firmly accustomed to using it with pulsating pressure. If you just pull, the horse will tend to 'lean into' the pressure, as is its nature. A horse that would try to flee once a large predator like a lion or wolf has gripped it with its teeth would risk deep tears to the skin whereby its inner organs might be exposed or even hang out, leading to certain death. Thus the horse feels the need to lean into the pressure and, at that very moment that the predator releases its grip for a second in order to bite in deeper, to flee – or to free itself with an effective kick. For this reason the entire basic training of a (young) horse is aimed at teaching it to yield to pressure applied by humans – be it when leading in hand, when picking up the feet, when tying it up, and so on.

Applying pulsating pressure that is gradually but steadily increased, and then immediately letting go and praising the horse once it obeys correctly, is the best way of teaching the horse. A second advantage is that you let your horse choose how strong the pressure should be before it reacts. You thus encourage it to think on its own instead of merely giving an instinctive reaction. In addition, you will find that as time progresses you will be able to ride with increasingly

The horse has to learn always to yield to pressure applied by humans and not to lean into it when it is being ridden. (Photo: Wentscher)

finer signals because, despite their considerable size, horses are very sensitive and, as long as they are not desensitised by rough treatment, react to minimal signs and the slightest of pressure.

Work on establishing rankings

The ideal equipment

For ideal results you can use either a well-fitted and tightly buckled head collar or a Dually training halter. This halter has been made very strong and has a wide contact area that, unlike the thin cords of a rope halter, does not painfully cut into the skin of the face or neck. The pressure of a bridle or of a chain across the nose bone is, in my opinion, too severe.

In order to be able to work with as finely applied commands as possible, I recommend using a lungeing rein. Neither lead ropes (with panic hooks that spring open when subjected to pressure) nor ropes with a heavy snap link are at all suited for finely given commands. A light but strong lunge rein with a tough whirl snap link is ideal.

A lunge rein is particularly effective when handwalking a horse proves to be problematic. If the horse charges forward, I can let it go for a few metres. With no permanent pressure on the neck, the horse will then relax slightly and I will be able to pull it firmly back towards me, without losing any of my balance or shifting my position.

Success through confidence

Particularly when working with horses that have been treated badly and kept in unnatural conditions and that have therefore lost their respect for a person's individual space, it is important to convey a high degree of self-confidence and to act consistently. This works best when you protect yourself adequately. It is definitely advisable, for example, to wear gloves that allow a firm grip without becoming slippery.

Wearing a helmet for groundwork will provide you with an additional sense of safety. Shoes with steel toecaps can prevent painful sprains and fractures to toes and feet.

Safety vests can also be helpful, as long as they do not overly restrict your movements. The better you are protected, the more confident you will be towards your horse.

Of course, safe surroundings are essential, too. You cannot move on slippery grass or in a muddy paddock with the degree of agility that is mostly required. A well-fenced-in area with a non-slippery surface will provide the best possible conditions for your work.

Success through the right learning atmosphere

A considerable contribution to the learning atmosphere is made by the trainer. At school we used to have ordinary teachers but also favourite ones – the latter were those with whom we had a very personal relationship because we felt they genuinely liked us and were interested in us or because we thought they could communicate their knowledge in a truly interesting, instructive, cheerful and yet focused way.

Although it is ideal to make a positive impression on your horse right from the start, you can at any time improve your later relationship still further by repeatedly conditioning your horse to achieve success by means of specially planned training sessions.

For this purpose, choose exercises that:
1. are easy for the horse,
2. the horse enjoys,
3. the horse finds easy to learn.

It makes no difference whether you train the horse from the ground or from the saddle. You can, for example, practise leading your horse forwards or backwards into its stable, or make it move each leg individually back and forth, so as to learn how to make it easier to manoeuvre on the ground. Or from the saddle you can practise trot-canter

A good mood is contagious and contributes to the team spirit! (Photo: Slowak)

transitions or shoulder-in in the canter, depending on the stage of training you have reached. What is essential is that you praise your horse frequently and warm-heartedly with gentle stroking and in a pleased tone. Even a riding school horse that is ridden by many other people can work more willingly just for you if it senses that you genuinely appreciate its efforts and achievements. You can thus condition a horse to aim at achieving success and at the same time strengthen your mutual team spirit.

If an exercise is not going well, it is sufficient merely to ignore the horse. Refrain from all punishment and replace it with consistently turning a blind eye. In the ideal case, leave your whip in the locker and concentrate on your own positive approach.

You will achieve the best results if you dismount as soon as an exercise has been successfully completed and you know that you cannot expect any further improvement on that day. If you particularly want to motivate your horse for some discipline – be it standing still, practising the flying change of leg or jumping a difficult fence – plan these exercises for the end of your training session and then, as soon as your horse has carried out its task, immediately dismount, praising it generously. Loosen the girth straight away and run up the stirrups. Then handwalk the horse until it has relaxed and cooled off and is able to return to the stable or field. In this way you provide the horse with an incentive to work hard and avoid all demoralising routine.

The right learning atmosphere for each individual horse

Lazy horses are usually a bit more animated and willing to perform when in unfamiliar surroundings. Horses with aggressive tendencies, too, are usually less self-confident and therefore friendlier when they are worked in a strange place. This will give us the chance to praise them more often and thus slowly improve our relationship.

Useful exercises

The following points are essential for all exercises: being over-enthusiastic does not help when learning new tasks. The smaller and more logical each learning step is, the better the horse can store it in its brain. If you praise your horse generously at the beginning, it will automatically connect this positive atmosphere with the exercise and carry it out willingly in the future.

As a golden rule, you should practise new exercises only on days when you feel fine and relaxed and are in a mood positive and patient enough to carry through the exercise as well as possible. The other days can be used to perfect those tasks previously introduced.

Correct leading to maintain ranking

The correct position when leading your horse is slightly to one side but distinctly in front of your horse and not at shoulder level. This will ensure the establishing and maintaining of your higher position in ranking. As the horse walks behind me and to one side, I can still observe it and its reactions out of the periphery of my eye.

The lead rope should be about one metre long and always slack, because the horse is not to follow me due to my pulling it along but because it always wants to walk behind me. The same goes for halting. The horse is to stop immediately and stand still at the same moment as I stop. The distance between us as I lead it enables it to stop without touching me – something many people are afraid of when walking in front of their horse.

Lead properly – in front of the horse, not at shoulder level! (Photo: Wentscher)

If the horse wants to overtake, it is helpful suddenly to change direction. (Photos: Wentscher)

Vary your technique in order to find out what your horse understands best and what costs you the least energy. If you stick strictly to these rules –especially with young and pushy horses or with those that question your ranking – many other problems will vanish as well, as though all by themselves.

Halting and standing still

As described above, the horse should halt and stand still immediately when we stop. You can help your horse by adopting an emphatically resolute and immovable stance, keeping your shoulders very straight. Ideally, the horse will not pass your shoulder. For the entire length of time that you spend standing still, your horse should do the same. Breathe deeply, and correct your horse in a friendly but determined manner if it does not stand quietly.

If the horse wants to overtake, a stern expression on your face at the right moment is often enough to make many horses change their minds. Before I resort to physical means, I prefer to try a threatening look to make it very clear that I on no account wish to be overtaken. If that is not enough, I will give the head collar a few firm tugs to make my meaning perfectly clear.

Another effective method, should your horse try to walk past you, is quite suddenly to change direction so that again you are positioned in front of it.

A resolute stance, shoulders straight – the horse has no alternative but to stop as well. (Photo: Slawik)

Speed variation

Walk your horse as described above and vary your speed and length of stride. You will be amazed at how well your horse can imitate you, because this is a situation that occurs within the natural herd as well. The exercise is perfect when your horse imitates every-thing you do without complication, even if you suddenly run off at a fast speed and then abruptly stop, whilst at all times the lead rope or lunge rein hangs loosely.

Lateral movements to develop travers, shoulder-in and other lateral work

Stand next to the horse's shoulder and, in pulsating rhythm, nudge it with your fore-finger at the place where the rider's side-ward driving leg action would be. Allow it a moment to understand the exercise but if it does not move, gradually increase the pressure until it reacts correctly. If you now draw its head by the lead gently towards you, your horse should step away from you with a correct sideways movement, ideally crossing its hindlegs, that is, crossing the near hindleg in front of the offside one.

Depending on how sensitive your horse is, a light snap of your fingers should be sufficient to induce this sideways yielding step; other horses will require a renewed pulsating pressure of the finger. Vary the pressure and after a while, if you have worked correctly, all that will be needed is a slight sign of the hand or a snap of the

With gentle nudges of the finger on the side of the abdomen, the foal will be induced to move its hindquarters sideways. (Photo: Maierhofer)

fingers in order to make your horse com-plete this lateral movement accurately. The aim is an exact 360-degree turn, performed around the inner foreleg on each side. This exercise will help you in difficult situations to regain control of your horse should it become agitated. This will, however, only succeed if the exercise has been well prac-tised beforehand and perfectly performed in varying locations. Do not overdo it, though: once the horse has learned this task, it only needs repeating now and then.

When moving backwards, the horse should arch its back and react to the finest signals. (Photo: Wentscher)

Reining back

Stand in front of your horse and put slight pulsating pressure on the lunge rein. Begin by exerting as little pressure as possible, that is, with no real pressure as such but just a 'tinkling' movement caused by the snap link of the lunge clinking against the ring of the head collar. This will be enough for most horses, because they usually react more willingly and better to less pressure and will tend to lean into an 'excess' of pressure. Praise your horse immediately as soon as it shows the desired reaction. Stop the 'negative' stimulus (the pressure) at once and stroke the horse's neck and forehead.

Then vary between one or several reining back steps. I am very meticulous about this exercise being performed correctly – as evenly and with as little sideways deviation as possible – exactly as I would like to have when actually riding. It is also desirable and the express aim of the exercise that the horse should not jerk its head up or move away with a hollow back, because, when ridden, the back should be arched, with the head carried not too high and the poll at the highest point. In other words, even when the horse steps back from us, it should not lose any of its nobility but remain full of expression, its steps elevated and its muscles correctly used.

That is why it is essential to begin with hardly noticeable pressure, and only if the horse does not react, very slowly and steadily to increase this pressure. Of course, your own temperament and energy is of tremendous importance for this exercise, too. When carrying it out, I take on the expression of an insuperable rock. You can practise that well when walking through a busy shopping precinct on a Saturday morning with heavy bags in both hands. Straighten your back and walk forwards calmly and with verve, a determined expression and the slightest of smiles on your face. If people give way to you, without you having to go round them all the time, you are ready for your horse. Should you crash into anybody, you will most likely have just met up with someone on the same wavelength with whom you could probably set up the most successful network.

Using-L-poles

Using poles in an L-shape exercises the concentration and co-ordination of the horse, as well as your skills in manoeuvring and in leadership.

Your horse should already have learned to move backwards when you apply slight pulsating pressure to the head collar or lunge rein. First of all, walk the horse forward through the lane made by the poles, and do this from both directions.

Then position yourself in front of the horse. With your upright posture and the

An upright posture encourages the horse to move backwards within the L-poles – do not forget to praise it afterwards by stroking its forehead! (Photos: Wentscher)

95

finest 'tinkling' or tweaking on the lunge in the direction of the horse's breast, make the horse step backwards. Keep sufficient distance between yourself and your horse. This is important because it must not be allowed to enter your personal space as you manoeuvre it, preventing it all the while from stepping out of the L or having to correct it once more by walking it forward. At the end you can lay a zig-zag course with the poles and/or gradually reduce the width of the lane between the poles and, here again, do the same exercise from the saddle once a good basis has been laid by your ground work.

Ground driving

Driving from the ground is an excellent exercise for establishing ranking and, in addition, a good preparation for horses not yet broken in. This exercise gives horses with riding problems or those returning to work after a long pause the best preparation for being ridden again with no difficulty. Psychologically, you are in your position behind the horse in that of the stallion behind his herd, driving it forward.

If you are still unsure of yourself or the horse is very bossy, it is to be recommended that you first work together with a helper who leads the horse by the head or just walks next to it. In any case, start in a secure, fenced-in arena before going out into the countryside or along a road.

In order to succeed it is imperative that your horse can be led from both sides. Use a Dually, a lungeing halter or an 'LG-Zaum' together with a padded girth and first let one of the lunge reins drag behind you. You have

When driving a horse from the ground, you are in the position of the leading stallion. (Photo: Wentscher)

It is advisable to teach the horse that a lunge rein dragging on the ground is not a source of danger. (Photo: Wentscher)

to be extremely careful when doing this – as it is always possible that you might lose a rein, it is of the utmost importance to get the horse used to this scenario while in safe surroundings in order to avoid a panic situation later.

Lungeing as a ranking exercise

Lungeing is beneficial not only for muscle development and keeping the muscles in form, as a warming-up exercise before rid-

ing, or as correct training, free from the weight of the rider. With the help of precise lungeing work, we can also establish our higher-ranking status indisputably.

Every time we deliberately drive the horse away from us, it will understand this, in terms of horse mentality, as an expulsion from our established twosome mini-herd. It makes no difference whether we do this while actually lungeing the horse or while we work with it in making it run free in a paddock or round pen. This reaction is very soon apparent in that every horse, very shortly after we begin to drive it away, will send out to us specific communication signals. It will lick and chew, lower its head, and of its own accord often attempt to make the circle smaller. Even horses that have to get rid of their bottled, up energy in those first minutes of release from the stable with excessive bucking and galloping will start to communicate as soon as fatigue sets in.

Establishing a ranking with lungeing will, however, only work if we have control over the horse. Just allowing the horse to race around the school is not at all what I mean, because it is our aim to dictate the pace and direction taken by the horse. Uncontrolled running on the lunge is also problematic in that it offers the horse the opportunity to practise its specific fleeing instincts. Ideally horses should only do this when no human is involved – and it must always be avoided during training sessions (race horses, of course, being the exception).

Indications of ranking problems when lungeing:

• The horse charges around us, changing pace and direction at will.

• It does not even begin to keep to the circle line, or it leaves it and constantly tries to come to the middle where we are.

• It does not move forward and blatantly ignores us.

• It tears off, out of all control.

• It charges towards us, rears or attacks us.

Each of these signals on the part of the horse has a specific reason behind it, and you must always check very carefully to see whether or not pain is the real cause before you are forced to realise that the hierarchy has not yet been clearly established or, indeed, that the horse is the leader.

Correct lungeing is as much an art as good riding and should observe the following aims:

1. Establishing the higher-ranked status of the person.

2. Correct exercising and training of the horse.

Lungeing can be used for the correction of arrhythmic paces, pronounced stiffness or laziness and also serves as an excellent way of releasing tension.

A plea for the double-lunge

I prefer working with the double-lunge at all stages of training or correction of a horse. Only work with two lunge reins gives me the possibility of initiating many correctly carried out changes of direction, and it is this feature in particular that gives the work variety and is so effective in training the horse's ability to concentrate. The value of the physical and mental effort required on the part of the horse is enormous. People forget far too often that the mental capacities of the horse, including its ability to concentrate, must be schooled. This cannot possibly be achieved to the same extent when working with one lunge rein alone.

The correct use of the outer lunge not only helps to exercise the horse on the circle line so that it retains the correct posture while on the bend, or to be more precise, causing the horse to bend while it moves in a circle so that its spine flexes and it tracks correctly with its hind feet. But by pulling gently on the outer rein, you also effectively prevent the horse from moving towards the centre of the circle.

As mentioned before, every lungeing exercise involves driving the horse away from its twosome mini-herd. In this, the question of ranking is not initially of prime importance the horse will always see the process of being driven away from us as a form of punishment. Many horses, especially young ones that still need to become familiar with this process, want to return to 'their' person

in the centre of the circle. This is not necessarily an expression of aggressive behaviour.
However, some horses, such as those that
when first put on the lunge were subjected
to violent lungeing methods, will perhaps as
a result have indeed developed aggressive
and defensive behaviour.

There are other horses that due to their
quasi 'anti-authoritarian' treatment, or confusing training methods from a horse's point
of view, have justifiably concluded that they
are higher-ranked than the human and, therefore, do not accept anybody's authority to
send them 'running round in circles'. This
behaviour can also be improved by the correct and appropriate use of the double-lunge.
An easy-to-read introduction to work with
the double-lunge can be found in my book
'Das Lernverhalten der Pferde' (Cadmos
Verlag, 2005). (Translator's note: the trans-
lated version of this book 'Learning Behaviour of the Horse' has not yet been
published.)

Horses that tend to bolt when lunged on a
single rein can also be successfully correct-
ed with a double-lunge. In this process it is
not only the effect of the outer rein, in my
opinion, that deals with the problem efficiently, but also the degree of concentration
that it demands of the horse. Horses moving
in a circle in one direction all the time and
only now and then being drawn into the centre of the circle for a rein change often get
bored and think out their own ways of how
to occupy their time. Working correctly with

Exemplary exercising of the muscles …

*… and the finest communication between
human and horse is achieved when training
with a double-lunge. (Photos: Wentscher)*

two lunge reins involves an exact study of
the horse's body language, thus it does not
purely exercise the muscles alone but also
has the quality of conducting the finest communication with the horse about what direction, in what paces, and with what degrees
of collection it has to go.

In order to achieve this fine communication by means of the slightest signs, horse and human have to work with intense concentration. A horse involved that deeply in such a task is faced with too much of a mental challenge to think about fleeing from the situation. Thus the correct and skilful use of a double-lunge can prevent various problems and challenges from arising right from the beginning.

Psychology of lungeing

Lungeing is a controlled expulsion of the horse from the established twosome mini-herd. The horse will regard this at first as punishment. In a natural herd, the stallion specifically trains his male offspring with rearing (exercising and strengthening the bending of the haunches and the co-ordination of the hindquarters) and pirouettes (turning on the hindlegs). Fillies are taught less to develop the hindquarters as to perform short, fast sprints in order to improve their speed when in flight. Thus it would seem that our horses are genetically encoded with a willingness to undergo physical training. The exercising intervals of the stallion are usually short but they might take place several times a day.

With lungeing you can observe the same non-verbal communication signals coming from the horse as it would give in the wild when driven away from the herd. It is important that we recognise and acknowledge them in order not to damage our friendly relationship with the horse.

If the horse keeps its inner ear pointed towards us, we can assume that it is focused on us. The ears and eyes of the horse are usually closely linked when taking in stimuli from the environment. This means that if the inner ear is directed towards us, the horse is perceiving us with its inner eye, too, and is waiting for our commands.

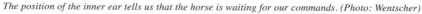

The position of the inner ear tells us that the horse is waiting for our commands. (Photo: Wentscher)

This can be seen as a sign of respect. Licking and chewing are always submissive gestures which, however, have the finest and most subtle differences in meaning according to context, if they are seen as 'humanised' emotive messages. Generally, we can assume that licking and chewing during and outside work sessions are an appeal to us to play it down.

Foals show a wrongly termed 'snapping' or 'smacking of the lips' behaviour (rhythmical opening and closing of the muzzle) as a gesture of meekness when, for example, they approach an adult horse and want to signal their submission and goodwill. This submissive sign effects that conflicts are to be avoided right from the start.

Other experts argue, however, that this licking and chewing is less a sign of submission towards another horse than a form of displacement activity for the foal itself, a way of relaxing and calming down.

A displacement activity in situations of stress works like a calming mechanism. By showing behaviour suggesting submission (like chewing or licking or lowering the head) which, however, has nothing to do with the actual stress situation, the horse interrupts the current flow of communication with the other individual and gives him a sign showing de-escalation of tension.

It cannot be decisively clarified whether a horse in licking and chewing uses this as a way of relaxing at the same time. Whatever the case may be, for us it is all-important to register these signs correctly, together with the emotional information they convey, so that we can react appropriately and continue our friendship and successful work with the horse.

The following statements – **in humanised language!** – explain what can be meant by licking and chewing in various situations:

• 'I accept you as ranking higher than me' (when the human enters the horse's personal safety distance).

• 'Please stop driving me away and let me come back to you' (when on the lunge or in a round pen).

• 'I am very friendly so please be friendly, too' (when the human approaches a timid horse).

• 'I am exhausted and need a break' (when on the lunge).

• 'Yes, I'll do what you want. I've understood' (when ridden or worked on the ground).

• 'Please take the pressure off' (a horse with saddle 'claustrophobia' being saddled).

• 'This is too difficult for me and I don't know what to do' (displacement activity).

• 'I have not understood properly' (displacement activity in situations in which a riding aid is given more and more forcefully but which the horse fails to understand).

• 'What I just did was wrong.'

• 'I am about to do something that I know is wrong.'

• 'Please stop it.'

• 'That hurts, it is very unpleasant.'

A horse's licking and chewing as non-verbal gestures on the one hand have to do with rankings, but on the other hand they can also be a plea to us to ease the pressure or to give an aid more clearly or in a different way than before, and they can even be expressions of pain or distress. In order to read their meaning correctly, the whole situation has to be taken into account.

If licking and chewing occur repeatedly during a working session, it is highly beneficial to our relationship with the horse that we respond and thereby assure it that we are, in fact, involved in a process of communication with it and are not just ignoring its fine signals. A sensitive dialogue between us and the horse is an imperative condition for a relationship that is successful and harmonious. A submissive gesture should be acknowledged by our easing the pressure (at least for a moment). The first and most subtle of signs on our part when lungeing the horse is a lowering of our eyes away from the animal's eye and towards the ground. Standing slightly at an angle to the horse, we could ask it for a lower pace if its message to us concerns its failing stamina. If it is more a question of an emotional signal suggesting that the horse wants the 'driving away' action on our part to stop, we can act as above or even in between times let it halt on the circle line, walk towards it and heap it with praise. It goes without saying that a horse that feels understood and respected will work far more willingly and better than one that considers its 'ideas' and needs ignored or overlooked. These small signs of affection and respect towards the horse can significantly improve your relationship and, therefore, should on no account be disregarded. Time and exact observation are the factors with which we can perfect the fine and subtle communication between ourselves and the horse.

We have to learn to perceive our horse's subtle messages and to react to them appropriately. (Photo: Wentscher)

Challenges facing the
human 'leader'

Horses live in a social herd organised around a hierarchy because it offers them safety and protection. If we want to have a higher rank in order to protect our horse in the same way, we have to be clever in our approach. Let us first take stock of a few considerations: the horse's senses are developed as finely as is essential for its survival as potential prey in the wild. Its sense of smell is significantly better than that of humans and is comparable to that of dogs. A horse can also hear better, especially sounds on higher frequencies reaching even to ultrasonic levels. This most likely also serves to make a more precise location of the origins of sounds possible. Horses in every part of their bodies are as sensitive as we are at our fingertips. In addition, they can sense the approach of impending earthquakes because their hooves detect the smallest earth movements, movements too minimal for humans to discern. Their eyes, too, are designed differently to the human eye and their lateral position in the head gives them a far wider field of vision, although they see most things with only one eye (monocular vision). When relaxed, their eyes usually focus on distant objects, rather than on details close to, so that they can register any far-off movements at once. A predator that has managed to get within a few metres' range is as good as sure of its prey. Horses are 'movement detectors' that notice the smallest changes in the distance, and they are also 'silhouette spotters' that remember previously encountered silhouettes and classify them as either harmless or dangerous. Each new silhouette or any change in detail to a familiar silhouette has to be re-evaluated according to one of these categories and stored in the brain.

These highly developed senses form the ideal equipment for an animal designed as prey that without any effective weapons with which to defend its life, such as horns, tusks, poison discharge and suchlike, first and foremost resorts to flight.

Seen in this light, it is therefore quite a challenge for us to establish our status as higher-ranked when so many of the danger signals and other sources of information concerning our surroundings remain completely or partly hidden from us. The primacy of the higher-ranked individual derives to a considerable extent from his vigilance and the ability to discern and analyse all the signs his senses convey to him.

The leading mare or the highly ranked members of the herd are distinguished by the extraordinary alertness of their senses and by their experience of potentially dangerous situations. On the alpha-mare abruptly raising her head, for example, the other herd members instantly recognise the presence of some potential danger and register her reaction – either a heightened awareness with all senses rapt and ready to flee, or a sinking of tension should the perceived object be deemed harmless. We can be certain that some horses consider us 'ignorant' because in their eyes we constantly expose ourselves to 'life-threatening' situations or approach objects that are potentially hazardous. This is particularly true for horses living or brought up in environments with few stimuli, which are, therefore, anxious and lack experience of real life. Horses kept predominantly in stables or those socially isolated do not have the opportunity to learn from other experienced horses what to be frightened of and what not. Also horses that did not experience a variety of different situations when they were young are more easily confused and scared by their sense perceptions than those with a comprehensive 'school of life' behind them. I am in favour of not starting to ride a horse before it is four years old. That does not mean, though, that it cannot and should not learn many things by that time. This is a question of management and also involves the expectations of buyers.

Although our senses are not as developed as those of a flight animal, we should still try hard to discern potentially fear-inducing stimuli before our horse does. This requires a very acute awareness when handling or working a horse.

In this it is helpful for you to analyse whether your horse is, for instance, particularly sensitive to noise, whether it shies easily at certain objects, or has problems with sudden movements. Depending on where its particular difficulties are, you can begin with desensitising it specifically in these areas.

Such an analysis is also important for you yourself to enable you to learn how to deal constructively and creatively with these reactions. Empathise with your horse and view the world as much as is possible and imaginable through its senses. Look into the direction of a noise or fix your gaze on a movement in the distance and then with a sigh of relief turn away from it. This will tell your horse that you have been alert and aware of the source of potential danger but consider it to be harmless, and with that return to concentrated work. The aim in such proceedings is a conscious and specific transfer of mood from you to the horse. If, for example, you notice an approaching tractor and become nervous because you do not know how your horse will react, you create with this very phenomenon of mood transfer exactly the opposite effect to that desired.

Your own (growing) nervousness projects itself onto the horse by:
• a heightened adrenalin level which the horse detects with its sense of smell,
• a heightened muscle tension that the animal feels, for example, in your fists stiffening on the reins,
• shallow, quicker breathing,
• hectic movements,
• a high-pitched voice in an unfamiliar tone.

With these symptoms we tell the horse that a potentially life-threatening situation is approaching or is already upon us and thus it should prepare to flee or even panic.

The fine art for us as the higher-ranked partner is to become aware of the new disturbance and then for a moment to relax our muscles, give a deep sigh of relief or even yawn infectiously in order to convey the

A nervous rider can cause the horse to believe it is in danger – and react accordingly. (Photo: Slawik)

harmlessness of the situation. The more convincingly your 'emotional language' can assure the horse that in spite of the unusual occurrence you are completely calm and relaxed, the sooner it will trust you and accept your decision as the leader. It is, however, of the utmost importance on no account to disappoint the horse in such a situation.

Mood transfer

Mood transfer is a conscious or unconscious communication of feelings, moods and (current) attitudes.

In the herd it is an important means for ensuring the survival of the individual. Should one horse show alarm because it has perceived something unusual (for example, a smell, movement or sound), the others will at once react to it, too, unless the horse, shortly after registering and localising the potential danger, relaxes once more. Thus almost all the horses are ready to flee at the same moment if the leader decides that flight is necessary.

A human can use this mood transfer to his own advantage in many situations by sending out distinct relaxing signals once he recognises that the horse has been alarmed by something. It is also important to understand in this context that the horse is probably not able to distinguish whether a person's agitation has been caused by anger, annoyance or fear – for the horse, it is only the degree of agitation that is decisive.

Mood transfer is, of course, not the answer to everything. With a horse that frequently shies or is generally frightened you should first check the conditions in which it is kept with a critical eye. Whenever possible the horse should be turned out with others and given the opportunity to learn as much as possible about its surroundings. A horse that is frightened of tractors will learn in a herd that a passing tractor is no reason to bolt. If we allow a horse to realise its flight instinct amongst companions, we will have less of a problem with it ourselves.

When riding or leading a highly strung horse it is to be recommended, if it is at all possible, that you prepare yourself mentally by self-inducing an absolute calmness of spirit and serene concentration. It is helpful to adjust your own breathing in that you consciously breathe in slowly and deeply. A further effective aid is to conjure up images or scenes in your mind that, when visualised, send you into a calm and tranquil mood. Most horses with a strong character only relax when you yourself project calmness and confidence. Some horses, however, do not relate to people well enough to be influenced by them. These are horses that have never had the chance to develop trust in people or whose trust has been damaged, for example, by the use of violence.

But, fortunately, most horses will, in fact, be affected by our mood transfer. The main challenge for us is to counter a horse's nervous anxiety with our own stoic coolness and composure. All horses will at once discern if our authority is not genuine, and it is therefore essential that you develop your own self-confidence to the extent that you radiate it wherever you go. It is also helpful in a stress situation to use the horse's naturally short concentration span and divert its attention by asking for a new task. In this way it is possible to re-introduce calm.

The more you work with your horse in a calm environment, whether riding or with ground work, the more 'tools' you will have available for dealing with any situation creatively. Even simple disciplines like reining back or moving sideways can help the horse to focus its attention on you once again. The most important thing is that you yourself find and project the calmness, confidence and degree of concentration that you expect from your horse.

If you do not know how to use mood transfer properly you will not be able to influence difficult horses positively. (Photo: Wentscher)

Frightened of 'ghosts'

If your horse shies easily or sees 'ghosts' in a certain corner of the indoor school, lead it past this trouble spot calmly. Another option is first to work your horse intensively, but also with very positive motivation, in another part of the school and then to let your horse have a break in the dreaded area. In most cases, the horse will not want to waste energy on shying if it is allowed to have a pause from hard work. If it does become agitated again, terminate the pause you had offered and resume work on the other circle calmly and with concentration. Then repeat your offer of a break in the problem area. Reward it with stroking and gentle words if it starts to relax. This way you actively work towards removing the problems from such places. If you punish your horse for shying just one single time by hitting it, jabbing your spurs in or shouting at it, you will intensify its fear and ruin your friendship and trust. Use your own superiority and proficiency; react as a supportive partner and not as a predator governed by instinct.

Learning to develop self-confidence

'Whether you think you can or whether you think you can't, you will always be right.'

Henry Ford

Humans unconsciously apply their own educational patterns acquired in childhood to horses. This can be a source of many problems because horses understand insufficient self-confidence on our part, or a complete lack of it, in a very different way.

We all have days when everything turns out well and we feel thoroughly satisfied with ourselves. We would not be able to recognise such if we did not have those other days when nothing seems to work. It is therefore helpful for all of us to remember some of the following proven methods for boosting our self-esteem at those times we feel unsure of ourselves:

1. Adopt a positive attitude towards yourself and your own abilities and trust yourself to be capable of even more. It requires a certain amount of discipline and sometimes a deliberate refusal to listen to negative inner voices. Negative attitudes like 'I can't' or 'I will never be able to' are usually self-fulfilling prophecies. Or is it that you expect reassurance from others? If so, do not let yourself become dependent on them; have the courage to trust in yourself!

A positive attitude – the basis for trust right from the very beginning. (Photo: Wentscher)

2. Create the physical and mental prerequisites. There is absolutely no substitute for training, extending your knowledge and working consciously on your own positive development. Even if it is sometimes more tempting to go for a coffee and a relaxing talk with your friends – your horse is an excellent personal trainer and a bout of grooming alone strengthens your arm muscles and creates a mood of inner satisfaction.

3. Do not compare yourself with others but concentrate purely on yourself. In this way you remain focused, with your eyes on your own personal goals.

4. Visualise situations and prepare in advance how to deal with them most intelligently. Devising good solutions beforehand will give you confidence; being caught unawares by a negative situation will weaken your self-respect.

5. Remain fair and objective towards yourself and accept the fact that you can make mistakes. Only people who do nothing will never make a mistake. Analyse the mistakes, learning from the experience, and then put them behind you as quickly as possible.

6. Create a group or join one and discuss your successes and problems together.

7. Set yourself realistic and achievable goals regarding your work with your horse and move towards them in stages. Reward yourself generously – as well as your horse, of course – for each single achievement.

8. Overcome your apathy (and/or laziness) and every day make yourself do something really special that brings you out of your shell. Even if the results are not always phenomenal, acknowledge your own courage and your ability in having defeated a negatively passive attitude.

Communication through energy

Energy, in the context of this book, has a mental as well as a physical factor. The degree of energy we radiate is based on our current fitness level but is also an expression of our mood and mental attitude. Other people around us react unconsciously to the specific energy we emit. Because horses lack the verbal communication of humans, they are masters in interpreting these vibes.

Our fitness and mental attitude determine the degree of energy we project,
vibes which the horse is very sensitively aware of these vibes. (Photo: Wentscher)

Energy is not a power that can be influenced from outside but is a strength coming from deep within us.

When overworked, ill, stressed, tired or emotionally unstable, we have less energy available than 'normal'. But if we are well-rested, fit and satisfied with ourselves, our energy potential is higher. When feeling out of sorts, irritated, nervous and exhausted, we emit negative energy (a nasty mood). In this way we send signals to those around us that we are at the end of our tether, and we retreat into our gloom. When we feel well, on the other hand, we radiate an inner and external spirit of friendliness, a positive energy, that attracts everyone to us and is contagious.

Horses are very susceptible to our specific current flow of energy. Therefore it is essential that we give this phenomenon our full attention. In particular, people who have unrealistic expectations of their horses, and automatically become disappointed, put an unnecessary strain on their relationship with these horses. Successful and experienced trainers have learned throughout the years to adopt the rule of planning the path to success carefully, and should anything not work out not to take it personally or be discouraged, because these mental attitudes are destructive and block all positive energy. Energy is also expressed by knowing what you want to achieve – it means being dedicated and focused on an achievable goal.

Horses sense very accurately whether you are sure of yourself or not and whether you know what direction to follow.

These energy principles can be universally applied to horses, too. A horse exercised only sporadically and spending 23 hours in a stable that is then taken out to be worked will at first have a lot of excess energy that is expressed by disproportionate shying and inattentiveness. But this will subside once it is allowed to let off steam. Due to their lack of exercise, these horses tend to have tense muscles that can, however, be relaxed in the course of a gentle workout.

Frightened or panicky horses can mobilise energy that can lead to complete hysteria. Other horses that have become dulled and resigned to their inertia (desensitised) can only be encouraged to show a good forward movement if an enormous amount of energy is invested plus the use of diverse aids. I have heard here in Germany of well-fed and well-cared for horses (that is, horses with a high energy potential) that have become so 'dead' that their trainers use electric shocks in order to trigger any reaction from them at all, because these horses no longer react in any way to normal spurs. (Horses become desensitised to mental and emotional stimuli, but never to pain.) This is the sad proof of how people are capable of destroying the emotional make-up of animals as highly sensitive as horses, and is an ugly violation of all ethical and moral obligations.

This face expresses fear and pain – this is a horse that people have mentally and emotionally destroyed. (Photo: Slawik)

Acquired helplessness

If a horse cannot carry out a specific task because it has not understood it, and if this happens repeatedly, the horse will finally resign. It perceives the situation as follows: it seems not to matter how it reacts. Nothing it does is right, and it is constantly ignored or even punished. In the end resignation sets in and it becomes passive. It is absolutely essential to offer the horse positive learning experiences, even when these are the smallest steps forward. As we have seen, learning is a process of one success leading to the next. Horses that never receive any positive feedback for their achievements, and thus never have the feeling that they are able to control or influence their situation in any way, will become apathetic and depressed. Above all things, through the use of violence the horse's basic need for control and safety, that it shares with people and other beings, will be utterly destroyed. This is why it is so enormously important when training a horse to offer it several options. The reaction that we desire from the horse should always be the easiest and most comfortable for it. Horses have an unmistakable feeling for whether they are being forced to do something or whether they have a choice. If the horse has the 'feeling' that it has a say and can influence its situation through its behaviour, in that it experiences positive or negative consequences, the 'free' decisions that it takes – either co-operation or the refusal to obey – will give it a sense of safety and control over that situation. The realisation that it has choices will encourage it to think about its behaviour and react accordingly.

Once a horse has reached the state of acquired helplessness, a seemingly hopeless situation, the development of psychosomatic and mental illnesses like stomach ulcers, stress-induced colic, neurotic disorders, etc, appears inevitable. Neurotic disorders are to be seen, for instance, in a heightened fear of objects, people or situations. If a horse has once reached this stage, without the help of therapy it will no longer be able to change its behaviour and will continue to evaluate new situations according to the old patterns. All learning capability will be severely impaired. The horse is literally broken and its psyche damaged. Once such a deplorable situation has set in, you have to see to it at once that the horse undergoes a positive learning experience. If you look carefully, you will always find something a horse can be rewarded for. You have to reduce your expectations far enough to give it the chance to do something right – no matter how small the task.

The right energy for nervous or highly strung horses

Nervous and highly strung horses should, of course, be observed carefully in order to determine the reasons for their behaviour. The composition of their hard feed and the amount they are given is just as relevant as the stable management. Isolated horses or ones that are stabled between horses they do not get on with will eventually show chronic stress symptoms. Horses that constantly experience pain, or that are asked to perform more than they can, become stressed and nervous, as do those that are immersed in what is considered to be animal love by their owners and are overly protected.

After standing for hours and hours in a stable, horses like to get rid of their excess energy explosively, a process that is utterly natural to them. Particularly in old-fashioned stables and riding schools that still have a 'rest day' for the horses, excluding all exercise, problems can be expected the following day.

But also in normal situations, for example, when loading, or with young horses that are faced with unfamiliar situations such as competitions or auctions, reactions from fear right through to panic can be seen.

In order to react properly, a person has to make sure that his own personal safety is guaranteed as far as possible. To be able to hold on to a horse that might bolt, it is imperative to wear non-slip gloves. If you have to let go of the lunge rein because of the pain

of holding it, serious accidents with the horse now running free can occur. Frightened horses out of control can easily stamp on people's feet; therefore it is essential to wear tough boots.

But even if you stand there in high heels and without gloves and with a horse that is bursting with nervous excitement in your hand, in the end what will help you most will be the stoic calm with which you react. Many people make the mistake of starting to shout, which makes the horse even more nervous and robs it still further of its sense of security. Instead, demand from your horse that it turns its attention to you, using small,

This young horse is carrying a rider for the very first time and thus is ridden with minimal body tension. (Photo: Slawik)

pulsating pulls on the head collar, lead rope or lunge rein. It is the constantly applied pressure on the line that in a panicking horse triggers the instinct to flee, so use only these short, pulsating pulls.

An experienced horse person will never let himself be infected by the nervousness of a horse but will counter the horse's tension with the greatest possible calm, control and objectivity. To do this, breathe in slowly and deeply and then sigh peacefully or even produce a wide yawn. Adopt a thoroughly relaxed or even slack body position as far as this is possible.

As soon as your horse realises that you have not joined in its anxiety, it can begin to put its instinctive behavioural repertoire behind it and start to assess the situation consciously. If you have established your higher rank definitively, you convey to your horse with your uncompromisingly calm attitude that it can also relax once more.

At the very first sign of any agitation, there are several things you can do to prevent the horse from panicking. Every time it clearly shows that it is frightened, you should avoid stroking it, though many people like to do so. This common reaction is very understandable and utterly human, but it will most likely be interpreted very differently by the horse: it will see the stroking as a reward for its previous or present panicky behaviour.

Of course, stroking is less damaging than punishing or hitting a horse for shying or jumping back or panicking, for that will only confirm the horse's fear. The best method, however, of training your horse to overcome most of its fear in the long run, is at the onset of any nervousness to ask it to carry out a specific task requiring it to focus 100% on the demands of this present discipline and thus eliminate all previous distractions.

Most horse owners are deeply emotionally attached to their horses and will easily become nervous along with the animal. Especially if you have had a bad fall or painful experiences when dealing with horses in the past, you will have good reason to be apprehensive in a difficult situation. Although these emotions are thoroughly understandable, only a calm and controlled attitude coupled with objectivity will get us out of such awkward circumstances. Bearing in mind that we have to set as good an example for our horses as we have to for our children, we see at once that we cannot make any excuses for shifting the responsibility from us. If you yourself are an anxious person or easily scared by your horse's reactions of fear and nervousness, you should first look for appropriate ways of (re)developing your own confidence when in the presence of horses or when riding and minimise all calculated risks. The best way is to find an experienced trainer to help you to learn how to overcome your own fear. Apart from that, constant work on developing your knowledge of horses further will always help you to strengthen your self-confidence when handling them.

In order to have a horse that is free of fear and will not shy easily it is best, above all things right at the beginning of the relationship, take it out regularly on rides into an unfamiliar environment and thus introduce it to new objects in a positive way, that is, to see to it that the horse does not begin to cultivate reactions of fear or panic in the first place.

Potential winners

> *Horse riding: 'The dialogue between two bodies and two souls with the aim of creating perfect harmony between them'.*
>
> Waldemar Seunig

Horses that suddenly explode at a competition usually have too much inner tension that they cannot otherwise release. (Photo: Wentscher)

Success in competitions can be planned – apart from your qualifications as a rider, the discipline to work towards a goal and to develop a strategy for this is immensely important. Successful horses have the right amount of routine, good nerves and ease on the one hand, as well as that correctly dosed, heightened adrenalin level needed for precision jumping or for performing a dressage test with extravagance.

Experienced horses that nevertheless still shy away from flowerpots, men's spotted ties or other insignificant features usually have too much tension within them which finds its explosive release at such moments.

In such situations, shying is not an instinctive reaction triggered by fear of a potential predator but a displacement activity with which the horse tries to release its bottled-up tension and nervousness.

A displacement activity is created by the inner conflict between two opposing instincts (flight or fight), or between an instinct (flight) and a learned reaction (carrying out a dressage movement).

The horse in the arena feels the rider's tension (or the general tension created by the spectators holding their breath and following the horse with their gaze) before or during the test, and due to the mechanism of mood transfer is alarmed, that is, ready to flee or fight. It has, however, learned that it is not allowed to flee from this situation and that there is no real predator to ward off. If the inner conflict is too intense, the horse has no other option but to release the tension in some way and it will shy at any object that

it would normally not even notice. Because of that, desensitisation to the specific object that triggered the shying reaction is not the prime means of solving the problem.

The rider has to learn to become less tense and exert a more calming influence on the horse. Additionally, the rider must raise the horse's tolerance towards a mass of spectators who, with bated breath and their bodies tensed, sit in the grandstand like lions about to crawl towards their prey. It is helpful to enter easier tests and more of them in order to minimise the pressure and gain a lot of positive experience, as well as to give your horse as much time as possible to compensate for its stress by relaxing at home in a field.

In order to stay mentally and emotionally balanced, horses need the chance to rollick about and enjoy their free time. (Photo: Slawik)

It is also important to create a positive association with competitions right from the beginning, that is, to turn them into experiences as enjoyable as possible for the horse. Ideally, you should take a young horse along several times when competing with another more experienced horse and generously reward it with attention and praise, and your own cheerfulness and inner calm will be contagious, as always. Of course, you can and should ride the young horse there, too – but only in places outside the arena, such as the practice area or, at the most, in tests in which you on no account ask too much of the horse and in which you ride without any unfamiliar, strong pressure. Everything should be as positive as possible. Stay away from hysterical riders in the practice area attempting at the very last minute to perfect their performance with the use of rough violence, or from people who are trying to force their horses on to transporters by hitting them, because in such situations your horse will be adversely affected through mood transfer. In order to make the competition situation as authentic as possible, you should plait the horse's mane beforehand and wear a show jacket and breeches, so that when the first 'real' competition comes everything goes just as cheerfully and smoothly. If you manage to convince your horse that competitions are generally a great day out, good results will follow naturally.

If you enter for tests but are yourself overly nervous, you can eventually transform even the most routined horse into a bundle of nerves, too. Take Bach Flower Remedies to calm yourself, and create your own mantra to reel off in your mind in order to convince yourself how little the whole thing affects you and how the entire competition scenario in any case is just one big bore.

The right energy for lazy horses

> 'Horses always understand a lot more than they let on.'
> Douglas Adams

Lazy horses in general, either due to their temperament or to their physical state, have less impulsion and less driving power than others. Some horses become lazy because they have become desensitised to their rider's driving aids which are given too often and with too much pressure, or are used at the wrong time.

The real cause of the horse's laziness must be detected and, above all, any underlying medical reasons ruled out. Some horses are very active when out in a field with companions but show no motivation whatsoever when ridden. With horses like these it is imperative to check the saddle because it is possible that the material with which it is padded has become matted so that hard lumps have formed, creating sore spots, or

Many horses have no other choice but to resort to 'laziness' when constantly subjected to roughly given aids. (Photo: Wentscher)

Other horses fail to show a powerful forwards movement because their riders have an unbalanced seat and thus disturb the horse's own very sensitive balance in the faster paces.

Yet other horses simply become confused by incorrectly given aids (wrongly timed) and are not prepared to help voluntarily at all because they have learned that they are unable to avoid whip or spurs anyway – no matter how they react. Wrong timing means that the rider continues to drive his horse forward either deliberately or unintentionally (through inadequate discipline or through insufficient balance and co-ordination) although the horse has already positively reacted to the given aid, for example, with a transition to an extended pace or a change to one of the faster ones.

Very sensitive horses try to teach their riders to give their aids more finely by not reacting to roughly given aids in the desired way but by being stubborn. Every horse wants to be ridden as sensitively as possible. It is often forgotten that a large animal like a horse can react to the most subtle signals (a motivating click of the tongue or the very slightest touch of the leg) and often, mistakenly, from the very beginning far too much force and pressure is used.

Certain horses also need a bit of time to react, and this should not be underestimated. Unfortunately, if a horse does not respond to a given aid within seconds, this can easily be mistaken for disobedience, upon which the

that the channel of the saddle has become too small for the horse and restricts its shoulder movement, or that the saddle quite simply no longer fits. A horse might tolerate the discomfort felt whilst walking, but not in the faster paces. It is as if we tried to run with a stone in our shoe or in jeans that are too tight: we might endure the uncomfortable feeling whilst walking slowly but we would not want to jog or run.

Many horses will not buck or rear when tacked up with saddles, bridles or bits that are ill-fitting or rub (as if they were used to suffering from an early age), but show their reluctance to work well with you in a different way, by restricting their co-operation.

command is repeated with more pressure. Such a scenario does not need to be repeated often before the solid foundations are laid for a horse with a slower reaction time to become increasingly dulled and desensitised.

A rider who uses his leg with more pressure when a horse fails to react promptly is like a person shouting a word louder and louder that someone else simply does not understand. This does not lead to a better understanding and is not a sign of competent communication skill. What is correct is to repeat the command with the same amount of pressure, as if the horse simply had not 'heard' or understood it the first time round. (More on this subject on page 122)

The specific reaction time needed by a horse has to be taken into account during training right from the very beginning and can be assessed through careful observation in its everyday situations. By conditioning the horse positively, that is, by rewarding it every time it reacts faster, you will be able to motivate it in the course of its further training to respond more quickly.

As in all situations that are slightly unusual, meticulous detective work on your part is required. Once you have eliminated health problems, ill-fitting tack or incorrect training as causes of the horse's laziness, you just have to face up to the fact that you are dealing with a horse that simply does not have much forward movement and that does not enjoy running fast. It might be a horse that still has the strong instinct to keep its energy reserves for exceptional situations. This type of calm horse

is often ideal for anxious riders or for beginners, so long as its character is otherwise good and it is well trained.

Generally, when dealing with a lethargic horse we need to invest more energy ourselves because we want to (re)sensitise such a horse and make it more responsive. Avoid all monotony in your work with such horses. Hacking out is a good option; most horses are more forward-going when out in the countryside. If a horse's general fitness is poor, a varied workload will improve it. This could include loose jumping along a jumping lane, working with poles and also cross-country riding, all in moderation and designed so that the horse thoroughly enjoys itself and does not feel overworked.

When working a lazy horse, our body tension will have to be higher than normal. At the same time, precisely timed aids are essential. We cannot sit with the same level of relaxation that we would have when riding a nervous horse, as we want to use mood transfer to project our heightened body tension on to the horse. This should not lead to a clenched cramping, of course, but it may certainly induce an increased muscle tone of the leg and body muscles. The aids must be given as finely as possible and the horse allowed an adequate reaction time before the aid asking for a more demanding task is given in a brief, precise and very clear manner (see also the box on page 122). During the rising trot you should try to be slightly ahead of the horse's movement and to stay slightly longer in the raised

To lengthen the horse's stride in the trot, we can stay in the raised position over the saddle just a bit longer and thereby influence the horse's movement positively. (Photo: Slawik)

position above the saddle to cause the horse to lengthen its stride and cover more ground.

If the horse has tried hard to work well, reward it immediately and remove all pressure. Initially, the emphasis is not on riding with correct contact but on doing everything to encourage a good forward movement and, within reason, to increase your horse's general fitness and enjoyment of movement.

When working from the ground we also move with well-accentuated and heightened body tension. The horse is a natural imitator that tries to equal the energy level of the higher-ranked individual. So set a good example, straighten your body and walk with strong, firm strides. Remember, however, to stay supple in the hips, to swing them (à la Marilyn Monroe), so that you do not appear cramped.

Teaching your horse obedience to the rider's leg

Anyone who trains young horses knows that no horse is born with practical 'speed buttons' on the side of its belly that only need to be touched by the rider's leg. Quite the contrary: young horses or those that are still raw will often tend to slow down when pressure or increased pressure is applied with legs or heels. This is on no account a sign of laziness or lack of sensitivity because these horses all react at once to a fly landing on the body.

The increase in pace as a reaction to the rider's leg pressure is, therefore, a learned reaction, and this learning procedure creates difficulties for some horses.

Using the methods described below you can train your horse quickly and unequivocally to learn (more) obedience to the rider's leg. And yet, as an advocate of horses' rights and of gentle and non-violent training techniques, I have great reservations about describing these tips because they require the use of a whip. A whip should be seen as a supportive aid; unfortunately, this view is upheld far too seldom in the riding world of today, and the whip is very often misused. No supportive device is good or bad in itself; it is the way in which it is used that is all-important.

So please bear in mind that the use of a whip as described and recommended here is only intended for this particular task and only up to the point at which the horse has learnt obedience to the rider's leg – ideally this should only take a few minutes. I am personally against all further use of the whip, both its routine use and its constant presence; with this in mind, I ask you to take seriously your responsibility as a role model for children and young people and also to spare your horse this permanent menace. If your horse is 'chronically' lazy, maybe it would be better suited to an inexperienced or less demanding rider. Most horses, however, will show good forward movement in response to only the finest commands and without the use of spurs or whip.

This is how you can condition your horse to obey very fine leg aids. A very light pressure with your legs should cause an immediate forward reaction. If this is not the case, then the pressure of the leg should at the very same moment be complemented by a gentle touch of the whip until a lively reaction follows. This must be rewarded at once by stroking and gentle words. At the same moment, release the leg pressure but ensure that the horse carries on at a lively pace (otherwise touch it again with the whip), and after it has done so, return to walk and praise it. The whole procedure must then be repeated and as soon as the horse reacts to the leg pressure immediately and correctly, omit the use of the whip and praise it again generously. It goes without saying that you must not use the reins as a 'brake' and thereby counteract the forward motion achieved. This method is on no account suitable either for riders who cannot (yet) keep their legs completely still and are therefore not able to communicate with very fine and precise leg aids, or for those whose constant, unfiltered leg contact with the horse's belly provokes nothing but misunderstandings in the process of communication. With very ticklish horses, maintain the leg pressure a little longer, and with lazy ones quick, brisk impulses of pressure can be applied with success.

The logic of this method results in it no longer being necessary to apply leg pressure to halt the horse, but instead to use stirrup pressure (downwards pressure briefly applied with the balls of your feet on both stirrups) in combination with the lower leg positioned back and the correct influence of your stomach and back muscles.

Sensitising with the help of the double-lunge

When sensitising a lethargic horse you will achieve the best results by introducing short-term changes to its daily routine. Interrupt the routine work schedule and for a few days do something completely different. Walks in-hand have proved to be successful, whereby you can both go jogging together if you like. Even a period of complete timeoff can work wonders if the horse is allowed to enjoy turn-out time with companions during which it has the opportunity to exercise itself as it wishes.

When you resume training, approach your horse in a new and different way from that of the past. If we consistently work towards achieving a heightened concentration and sensitivity, we will end up with a horse that is very willing to co-operate with us. It helps if you restrict the normal riding and lunge-ing routine in favour of introducing alternative activities. If you do not want to go without riding, choose to hack out and ride different routes or transport your horse to a different environment and ride there. Horses learn in association with a particular context, that is, if you always train in the same location, your horse will maintain an unchanging mental approach to its work. If, however, you have the possibility of training it somewhere else, you will often achieve better results. Concentrate on your ground work carried out in short, positive sessions. Everything that arouses your horse's atten-

tion is permitted. Practise giving commands precisely, during which you develop your skill in using the finest body signals right through to touch-aids that are gradually intensified if the horse fails to respond. Reward your horse for every correct reaction with expressions of your sincerely heart-felt appreciation, such as gentle stroking and words spoken in a soft, loving voice. In this way you let the horse experience its own success and, at the same time, it gains the motivation to make even more of an effort to please you. Once your horse willingly begins to co-operate with you because of these positive experiences and begins to react to aids given more finely, continue by introducing short spells on the double-lunge.

Here, too, you must keep to a finely-tuned system. The principle here is: the sooner the horse reacts, for example, moving into trot at the very first command to do so, the sooner it is allowed to go back to walk again and is thus rewarded for its immediate reaction. The more your commands have to be repeated or the intensity of aids heightened before your horse reacts, the longer it is kept working.

This type of work is not aimed at improving the horse's general fitness but merely serves to heighten its sensibility. This means instant easing of the pressure after every immediate and correct reaction, and persistent continuation of pressure until the requested reaction is shown at once. If this is carried out consistently and correctly, the horse will no longer ignore your commands but

Work with the double-lunge that is carefully planned and applied with concentration
can contribute greatly to improving the horse's sensitivity and speed of reaction.
(Photo: Slawik)

willingly work with you. Keep steadfastly to this method until it works with absolute certainty before you ask the horse to perform more difficult tasks, and never let it become routine. If you make the horse canter for three strides before it is permitted to go back to walk or trot, make it seven strides the next time, and the time after that five. Do not become predictable, because your horse must not be allowed to anticipate and react of its own accord to commands not yet given. Once you have re-established sensitive communication, apply the same principles when riding. It is ideal if you have the chance to ride other horses that react promptly to correctly and finely given aids so as to enable yourself to develop a feeling for this once again.

Conclusion

Dear Reader,

I would like to thank you for accompanying me throughout these past pages and taking a closer look at the enthralling world of the horse's life and mind. It has enriched my life so much to be able to show horses the 'easy' way and to practise this school of thought with them, together with my highly valued students. For me, the process of finding out more about horses and their psyche, but also about our own shortcomings in our dealings with them, is to be seen as an active step towards protecting animal rights.

I have shared with you, insofar as this is possible in a book, my personal conviction that active, positive leadership is the key to a harmonious relationship with our horses. I see self-discipline and the development of one's own understanding and skills as a matter of course and as an expression of self-confidence and strength.

In my opinion it is not enough just to instruct riders in technical facts, because a successful partnership with a horse begins with and within ourselves, and it involves acquiring a thorough knowledge of the social and emotional world of the horse. This book makes an important contribution towards this, and you will be able to profit from its compiled thoughts and findings again and again, as long as you keep your senses alive and your mind open towards horses, and as long as you are prepared to work towards seeing the world through their eyes. With this I would like to wish you every success in bringing out all that is best in your horse and its personality, both in your work together and in your relationship as a whole, and also that this glow will reflect back on you so that you will always be greeted with a look saying, 'I'm so glad you're here – and what are we going to do today?'

Linda Weritz

OTHER CADMOS BOOKS

Birgit van Damsen
Improving Performance

This book discusses the possible causes of a lack of motivation – from physical problems, incorrect feeding, to permanent under- or over-demand of the horse, and it outlines solutions that can recover a seemingly hopeless situation.

Paperback, 80pp, fully illustrated
978-3-86127-956-3

Claudia Götz
Free Jumping –
A Practical Handbook

Using this practical book, which contains many helpful illustrations, the reader will gain a better understanding of how to prepare for and carry out free jumping, and develop an eye for the horse's general improvement during training.

Paperback, 96pp, fully illustrated
978-3-86127-954-9

Hans-Peter Scheunemann
Starting out in Eventing

This book, by an experienced trainer, judge and course designer, describes all the the important requirements for safely improving your horse's ability in the cross-country phase. Training programms and instructions for coping with specific cross-country obstacles are included.

Paperback, 144pp, fully illustrated
978-3-86127-957-0

For further information:
Cadmos Books c/o Vicky Tischer
13 The Archers Way · BA6 9JB Glastonbury
Phone 01458 834 229 ·E-Mail info@cadmos.co.uk